THE CONTINENTAL

LANDSCAPE ANNUAL

OF

Europan Scenery,

EDITED BY

FREDERICK FERGUSON, Esq.

ILLUSTRATED BY

NUMEROUS HIGHLY-FINISHED ENGRAVINGS.

1835.

LONDON:

PUBLISHED BY H. RILEY, ST. JOHN STREET,

AND THE BOOKSELLERS OF PARIS, VIENNA, ROME, ST. PETERSBURGH, BERLIN, AND ALL THE EUROPEAN CITIES.

ONE GUINEA.

ISBN
9781406990218

W0010025

LONDON:

PRINTED BY J. TRAPP AND CO. 31, BUDGE ROW.

ADVENTURE IN MANTUA.

" I can call spirits from the vasty deep."

It was one evening in the latter end of October, 1810, that I was left about an hour before midnight, almost alone, in one of the public rooms of the principal hotel in Mantua. The apartment was spacious, and its size seemed augmented by the scarcity of inmates. A man of apparently spare habits, habited in somewhat rusty garments, and whose general appearance was much below that of the company accustomed to frequent the house, was my only companion. The fire was low, and the candles glimmered dimly in the extent of the room. I had looked in turns over the Gazettes, which were scattered on the tables, and began to think of retiring. I endeavoured to gaze out of the window, but the night was pitchy-dark, and no object was discernible, except where the lamps, attached to the public edifices in the street, made half visible the ill-defined masses of buildings. I sunk back to my seat by the dying coals, and perplexed myself with weighing the comparative advantages of departing to my lodgings, or remaining at the hotel for the night. The clock struck, and I found it was within a quarter of the witching hour. The stranger had not yet spoken, nor was I inclined to break the silence; at length my companion spoke.

B

" I think, sir," said he, " that in the debate which took place this evening, you inclined to the opinion maintained by the Signor Ripari ?" There was something in his manner and the tone of his voice much superior to what I should have expected from his appearance.

I answered him in the affirmative.

" Your reasonings, then, do not induce you to believe in the possibility of the appearance on earth of a departed spirit, or at least in the power of such a being to make its presence perceptible to human creatures such as ourselves."

" I certainly am not guilty," I replied, " of presuming to assert that such a revisitation is beyond the limits of possibility; probability, I own, the opinion in question appears to be devoid of."

" True; argument is against the hypothesis."

" I know but one in favour of it—the general assent of all ages and nations to the reappearance of the dead."

" I do not think," said he, " that much strength is to be acquired from that argument, considering the state of the earthly inhabitants of the world ; their confined reasonings and mental investigation—their consequent wonder and astonishment at many of the operations of Nature, which, though now familiar, were to them inexplicable, may account for the use of a notion, which, when once conceived, would be eagerly embraced and widely disseminated. Argument, therefore, I may repeat, is entirely against the credibility of the opinion."

PREFACE.

THE objects of interest on the European continent are much more numerous than is generally supposed, and it is a matter of great surprise that so few Engravings of them have been submitted to the public : to remedy the deficiency is the object of this publication, and it is presumed will, in a small degree, fill up the vacancy occasioned by the withdrawal of one of the best of the Annuals containing Views. A departure from the usual custom has, in this Volume, been adopted, that of omitting the names of most of the subjects, for the sake of affording travellers and others acquainted with the places the pleasure of recognising them; also of adding to the interest of the story, by the " *imagining what a sort of place it is,*" of those who are not acquainted with the locality of the scene of the tale.

CONTENTS.

ADVENTURE IN MANTUA ....Page   1

THE STUDENT OF GOTTINGEN   10

NICHOLAS PEDROSA, THE BARBER OF MADRID   34

THE ELOPEMENT; AN ITALIAN STORY   59

THE TWO RINGS; A TALE OF FRANCE   69

THE HUNCH-BACK COBBLER OF VENICE   87

THE BROTHERS OF DIJON   114

THE PHYSICIAN OF MILAN; OR THE COUNTERPARTS ..   130

THE RUIN OF THE ROCK; A SPANISH STORY   142

EDELIZA; A TALE OF THE FRENCH COURT   154

THE THREE BEAUTIES OF DRESDEN   172

THE LOVERS OF LYONS   188

THE MERCHANT OF BREMEN   209

THE PRUSSIAN, AND THE BRONZE STATUE   256

THE MARRIAGE GIFT; A GERMAN STORY   267

ZERLINA, AND THE OWL OF THE ARNO..............   280

" In that case," I replied, " the question must be considered as settled, for by what means, except argument, are such enquiries to be prosecuted ?"

" You do not, of course, consider arguments, or the conviction arising from them, as the only sources of belief?"

" Certainly not; belief may originate from numerous causes : for instance, from the retention of what has been shewn to us by experience."

" It is upon that very cause that I ground my belief in the reappearance of the forms of the dead."

" Then you are a believer ? But do you think that the testimony of another's experience can overcome the improbability of the alleged instances ; especially since the pretended beholders of apparitions are generally weak and ignorant persons, and likely to be the subjects of delusion ?"

" Passing over," answered my opponent, " the incorrectness of your statement, and the sophism of the argument you would insinuate, your observation is founded on an assumption unauthorised by any expression of mine."

" But where : how ?"

" When I spoke of experience, I said nothing to confine it to the experience of others, consequently, testimony is out of the question."

" You do not, surely," I answered, " proceed upon your own experience."

There was a sort of half smile on his features, as he replied to my question, " Why not ?"

I started with surprise.

" You have been favoured, then, with a communication with the world of spirits ?"

" I have."

" When—where—how ?"

" The narration would be tedious," he replied ; "if your inclination lead you, you shall yourself know as much as I do."

" That is to say, you possess the power of calling these mysterious existences to the sight of yourself and others ?"

" Come and see," was his reply ; and leaving his chair, he seemed about to depart. He lingered, as if waiting for me to accompany him.

I feigned a laugh, and said, " that my faith in his power was not so firm as to induce me to leave the house at so late an hour."

" True," answered the stranger, " it grows late ; 'tis past midnight—you are doubtless remaining here—and I will therefore bid you farewell ;" and bowing with great politeness, he was gone before I could speak to detain him.

A strange and fretting discontent seized me; I was vexed that I had let him depart, and lamented that I had lost such an opportunity of extending my knowledge beyond the limits of the visible world. It may appear singular; it did so to me afterwards. I knew that I felt no doubt of the truth of what my companion had asserted ; on the contrary, I did not even revolve it as a thing whose reality was to be established, but thought and acted upon it as a settled truth. Yet I had only his bare word for so wonderful, and apparently incredible a tale. He was a stranger to me, and our connexion arose from one of the most commonplace casualties of life—the meeting in a coffee-room. So it was, however; I believed implicitly in what I had heard.

I retired to bed—sleep I had none—and when, after a lapse, as it appeared, of many hours, I caught a glimmering of the sky, I sprung from my restless couch, dressed myself, and rousing the servants to let me out, rushed into the street.

I paced round the city with eager steps, examining every countenance I met, and searching, though in vain, for the stranger of the preceding night. I blamed my own carelessness in not ascertaining his name, and hastened back to the hotel, to inquire from the waiters who he was. Of this, however, they knew as little as myself; they only remembered having occasionally seen him; but with his name, or any other particulars which could guide me in my search, they were unacquainted. I hastily dispatched my breakfast, and again commenced my wanderings.

At length, when the eagerness of my researches had wearied and irritated me, as I was crossing, in great haste, one of the squares, I ran against some one, and upon turning round to apologize, found my labours at an end.

"You are not the first," said the stranger, half-laughing, and seeming fully aware that he was the object of my pursuit, "who has looked diligently for a something that lay just before him at the time."

I felt, I know not why, half-ashamed of acknowledging the cause for which I had sought him. I recounted to him the history of my rambles, and we talked on different subjects.

" And so," said he at length, upon a pause occurring in the conversation, " you have risen before day, and run about till noon, to find a man with whom, when found, you have no business but to tell him how diligently you have looked for him."

I blushed and hesitated ; he smiled as he spoke, and this increased my confusion.

" Excuse me," I said ; " I have other business."

" Indeed ! Pardon my freedom ; but had we not better dispatch it without delay ? You will allow me to inquire the nature of it ?"

" To tell the truth," I replied, " I have been thinking since I saw you last, of the subject which then formed the ground of our discourse."

" Oh ! I remember it was of the reappearance of the dead, of ghosts, ' of those subtle intelligences which accommodate themselves to shapes, unite with sounds, present themselves in odours, infuse themselves in savours, deceive the senses, and the very understanding.' Was it not so ? What think you of St. Austin's description ? Is not the holy father a strong authority for our side of the question ?"

" The fathers of the church were men, and not infallible. But our talk was of the existences you speak of."

" I made an offer to you at the time, which you rejected," said he.

" Is it too late to avail myself of it even now ? Cannot the error be retrieved ?"

" On one condition."

" Name it."

" That when you have seen what I have to exhibit, you will ask no questions concerning my search. I demand this," he added, "more for your own sake, than to gratify any disposition of my own. I wish not to conceal knowledge, where the promulgation of it can benefit the world : that which I peculiarly possess, is a curse rather than a blessing."

The manner in which this was said, disposed me to think favourably of the speaker. I felt convinced he was sincere. I made the promise required of me, and taking his arm, I walked with him to the house where he informed me he lodged.

He led me into a small room, plainly, though not inelegantly, furnished. A moderate-sized bookcase, with shelves, well filled with antique-looking volumes, formed the most prominent among its accommodations. There was nothing placed to be seen, no ostentation of science, nothing but what the apartment of any private man would have exhibited.

We so naturally associate the idea of darkness, and seasons of solitude and stillness, with that of the visions of the deceased, that I was astonished, when, after we had been seated a short time, my companion asked if I was prepared to name the person I most wished to see? I communicated my thoughts to him. He answered, " All times are alike to me, and a spiritual existent knows not the distinction of light or darkness. We will therefore postpone it ; speak, when you wish me to fulfil my promise ; and, in the meanwhile, we will pass

the time by looking over a few of my favourite authors;"
and he unlocked, as he spoke, the glass-doors that sheltered his volumes. He spoke of the authors that we
opened, like a scholar and a man of feeling. I was delighted with his remarks, and had almost forgot the
object which had led me there, when the deepening
tinge of the sunbeams shining through the casement
warned me of the approach of evening. I was ashamed
of having so long delayed, fearful of the imputation of
irresolution. I shut the book I held, and looked at my
unknown acquaintance. A look was enough for him.

"Be it so," said he; "name the individual, and he
shall appear."

We were arrived at a crisis——a fearful one I felt it.
The firmness, which a moment before I flattered myself
that I possessed, vanished at the near approach of the
moment which should place me in contact with a being
of another nature; one too, whom, of all the creatures
of the earth, I had known, and loved, and cherished.
I felt a fearful oppression of the heart, my limbs were
chill and trembling, and the power of speech well nigh
deserted me.

My conductor observed my confusion, and begged to
defer the experiment, or to abandon it, if I wished, altogether. I refused to postpone it, and summoning all
my strength, I loosed the bonds that enchained my
tongue, and spoke the name of the dead.

Oh, God! I spoke *her* name, and she sat before me as
when on earth, as beautiful, and those eyes so deeply
dark, shining upon me with all the gentle fire, the fond
affection that illuminated them in her days of youth and

earthly blessedness. I strove in vain to touch her hand
—to feel if what I saw was indeed my—I dare not write
the word,—or but a dream—a vision; and the face
smiled a melancholy smile, and the eyes shone, and the
lips moved—she spoke! I felt that voice again; I
shrieked her name, my eyes were blind, my limbs were
nerveless; but my ears for a moment drank in the
heaven of that sound, as I fell, void of sense and consciousness, to the earth.

At length I recovered, and leaving the room, I
descended into a garden by which the house was almost
surrounded. I leaned against a lime-tree, and looked
round on the peacefulness of nature. My thoughts
were with other and happier times, my meditations were
sad, but not bitter; there was one image had been pain-
fully recalled to my memory, and a thousand fond asso-
ciations startled up and played around the recollection.
I was startled from a reverie like this by the sound of
an approaching footstep. It was a servant of the house,
who delivered me a letter, which I read as follows:

"I have performed my undertaking; do you remember the obligation of my promise? It is near to impossible that we shall ever meet again. If it should happen otherwise, remember you are to make no inquiries.
Speak no word of this to any one, forget what has been,
and be content. Your friend ——."

I was dissatisfied and uneasy. I inquired after him,
but could obtain no information of his name, occupation, or residence.

I left Mantua the day but one following, and returned
to England.

THE STUDENT OF GOTTINGEN, AND THE SABLE CLOAK.

" If that thou be'st a devil, I cannot kill thee."

OTHELLO.

AMONG the youthful students of Gottingen, none were so handsome, so amiable, or so miserable, as Carl Wilstadt. The poor fellow was in love; and that will sufficiently, and most abundantly, exemplify the truth of his misery; for the little god, Cupid, almost invariably renders his votaries wretched ; sometimes bestowing future happiness with additional zest, but more frequently leaving them heart-broken and discontented, for the remaining period of their joyless existence. And such promised to be the eventual fate of poor Carl, who, though looking for the future with sanguine hopes, yet could discover but little prospect of success to his love for years to come. He was the son of a wealthy merchant of Hamburgh, who, wishing to bestow on his son that of which no future misfortune could wholly deprive him, had sent him to complete a long course of studies at the university of Gottingen, provided with several letters of introduction; one of which introduced him to a being, on whom he speedily felt his future felicity or misery depended.

Caroline Hernsdorff was the daughter of a rich merchant, who having acquired a very large fortune, had retired from the fatiguing turmoils of trade, and resided, with his young and beautiful daughter, at a pretty villa, a short distance from the university. The house of Mein Herr Hernsdorff, Carl had visited shortly after his arrival at college ; Caroline saw nought to dislike, and much to admire, in the handsome young student; and her father, to whom he sedulously sought to play " the agreeable," likewise admired him : thus a hearty invitation was given by one party, and as eagerly accepted by the other.

Time passed on—and nearly two years had elapsed since his first arrival at Gottingen ; and Carl felt that, if his store of learning was increased, his heart was irrevocably lost ; he doubted much if Caroline returned his passion, although one more versed in such matters than our student, would have entertained no doubt upon the subject. It was one evening, on returning from a somewhat extended visit, that Carl began to meditate seriously upon the subject.

" Does she love me ?" was the question which he asked himself ; and whilst he would fain think " Yes," Fear sternly shouted " No !"

" True," he considered, " she has refused several advantageous offers since I have known her, and she treats the crowd of admirers by whom she is surrounded with undisguised contempt ; but then it by no means follows that it is because she loves me."

Thus did Carl vex and perplex his mind, until he finally resolved to make his doubts certainty, on the following morning, by disclosing to Caroline his passion, and relying on her partiality, if any she had for him, for a favourable decision.

On the following morning, Carl dressed for this important visit with zealous care; and having contrived to display his really fine figure to the best advantage, he bent his way to the villa of Mein Herr Hernsdorff. Many things passed over the mind of Carl as he paced along; and among them, the recollection that his father must be consulted ere he could marry; but about this he cared right little, for Carl had ever been a spoilt boy, and doubted not that his father would willingly comply with any wish of his.

Attached to the villa was a large and beautiful garden, in which the fair Caroline spent much time; and as Carl wished to gain her consent, if possible, ere he addressed her father, he determined to enter the garden, and seek her there. The wall was neither high nor difficult; and Carl speedily found himself approaching the shady bower in which Caroline loved to recline. The day was delightful: the sun shone joyously, and the garden, dressed in the beauteous garb of summer, raising his spirits, inspired the breast of the student with somewhat more confidence. As he reached the bower, the sound of sobbing from within amazed him; and entering, he found Caroline sitting in a dejected posture, weeping bitterly. She did not see him, and he stood for a moment without moving; at length,

" Gracious heaven! what is the matter?" burst from his lips. A scream escaped her, as she rose from her seat, and, with averted looks, attempted to leave the bower.

" Stay, stay, I entreat you," he exclaimed, seizing her hand. It was withdrawn ; and, somewhat angrily, Caroline said,

" You might, sir, methinks, have intruded somewhat less abruptly;" as she spoke, a miniature which she had vainly endeavoured to conceal, dropped from her hand ; and as Carl stooped to raise and restore it, an action which she attempted to prevent, a slight glance assured him that it was his own features. It dropped from his grasp ; and catching the fair hand which had been extended to conceal the miniature from view, he covered it with kisses. Glowing with blushes, Caroline heard the impassioned words of her lover ; and when he paused for an instant, to await her reply, she said, as calmly as her feelings would permit,

" Carl Wilstadt, I am betrothed !"

Any words but these, Carl could have heard with comparative hope : a final rejection his continual love might have shaken ; but this cruel information, for a moment dashed all his hopes of happiness to the ground. A pause ensued : Carl still retained her hand, and stood before her with his eyes fixed on the green sward at her feet.

" As such is the case," she at length continued, but with faltering tongue, " the sooner we end this painful interview the better. Farewell! fix your affections on one who, unbound by other ties, can return them with the fervency they merit."

She would have now retired ; but Carl held her hand so tightly that she could not possibly disengage it.

" Tell me," he said, as those sanguine hopes which

youth invariably bestows, rose once more in his breast, " tell me, was it with your own consent that you were betrothed ? do you love him to whom you are promised ?"

" Alas !" she replied, " I never saw him ! my father promised me in marriage to the son of some old friend, when I was scarce six years old, and he has told me this morning that my intended husband will be speedily here to claim his wretched bride ;" and a fresh burst of tears followed.

" Then," exclaimed Carl eagerly, with shortened breath, and speaking in disjointed sentences : " you— you do not love him—you would avoid this marriage, Caroline," and he sank on one knee, " I adore you : say, oh ! say, that you return my love ?"

Still with averted looks, and whilst her hands trembled in his, she answered,

" Of what use would be the confession—and yet— oh, Carl !" she sank into his arms, and he boldly impressed the first seal of love upon her ruby lips. A few moments passed in rapture, and then came cool reflection, and then the recollection that the chance of their eventual happiness was small indeed.

" Go, Carl," said Caroline, with assumed fortitude; " you must hasten away, and never think of me again."

This speech, it will be readily believed, had little weight, when addressed by a handsome girl of eighteen to one for whom she had just confessed her love.

" Indeed, dear Caroline," answered Carl; instead of giving way to such gloomy ideas, let us rather think

of some plan by which we may prevent our mutual un-
happiness; for believe me, love, I will never see you
in the arms of another and live;" and then followed a
most animated discussion, which was terminated by
the near approach of Mein Herr Hernsdorff, seen
through a vista of the garden, before they had come
to any decision: Carl spoke quickly, and in a low tone.

" I will write to my father, and supplicate his inter-
ference; should that fail, I will shoot my rival and fly
with thee."

Caroline had no time to utter a single objection to
this feazible plan, for her father appeared almost immediately; his surprise at finding Carl in the garden
was naturally great, and his questions as to how he
had obtained entrance might have proved somewhat
troublesome, had not the present of some peculiarly
high-flavoured tobacco, which Carl had had the fore-
thought to bring in his pocket, satisfied the honest
German. The student soon took his departure, under
the pretext that some difficult problems required his
immediate attention; and, in fact, he was not far from
the truth, although the problem which he wished to
solve, viz. how to obtain Caroline, appeared far more
difficult than any thing the whole course of mathema-
tics could produce. A gentle whisper informed Caroline, that he would never relinquish her; while, at the
same moment, he intreated the name of him to whom
she was betrothed? This Caroline could not inform
him, even had she been inclined, as the name of her
betrothed husband was wholly unknown to her, and
Carl bent his way towards his solitary chamber in the

university.   A letter from his father awaited him here, which contained the agreeable intelligence that he had fixed upon a lady to whom he had promised the hand of his son, and that he should be with him on the following day; concluding by desiring him to make arrangements for immediately returning with him to Hamburgh, in order to settle all preliminaries.   This unfortunate letter rendered Carl completely wretched; he well knew that his father, though fond of his child, was extremely firm in his resolves, and as the promise of his hand had been made, he felt that to expect his father to break that promise would be worse than absurd.   He paced his little chamber in a perfect frenzy, and Carl at this moment was probably the most handsome, certainly the most miserable student in Gottingen.

He threw himself on his couch, and tried to fix upon some plan to pursue.

" If she would fly with me," he half muttered; " no, my father will never forgive me—her father will never pardon her, and then comes starvation."

He started up, and rushing into the streets, paced wildly along; his hurried actions excited much attention, as almost without intention he turned his steps towards the villa.   When within sight he paused, and not knowing what excuse to make for his sudden appearance, entered the deep shade of one of those ancient forests for which Germany is famed, and which flourished " in most admired disorder," at a little distance from the dwelling of Mein Herr Hernsdorff. Here throwing himself at the foot of an aged tree, he determined to await nightfall, and then under its friendly concealment, endeavour to gain a private interview with his beloved. Covering his face with his hands, he remained for some time lost in thought: from this reverie he was, however, awoke by a sneeze at a little distance. Unaware, as he had been, that any mortal was near, and starting from his position, he looked round and discovered, within a few yards, a figure approaching towards him. The sun was rapidly sinking in the horizon, but his last beams yet glancing among the trees, discovered to him perfectly the form of the stranger. He was about the middle age, tall and stoutly built, his complexion of a clear brown; his eyes bright and keen, and his lips wearing an habitual sneer of contempt. This personage wore a black hat, with a plume of overhanging feathers, and from his shoulders depended a large and ample cloak of sable hue, which being wrapped somewhat tightly around his large yet not ungraceful figure, shewed nothing of his under dress. He advanced, and bowing politely to Carl, threw himself carelessly on the turf, and remarked on the warmth of the weather.

In his present frame of mind, Carl felt by no means inclined for trifling conversation; and to no description of being, save the one who now addressed him, would he have vouchsafed an answer. There was, however, a certain something, perhaps of concealed dignity, or of condescending affability, as though the speaker was aware that he communed with one beneath him, in the manner of the person who now addressed him, that forced an answer, and he said—

c

" The sun now sinks rapidly ; a few moments more, and having withdrawn his beams, the air will cool.''

" All this I know,'' calmly replied the stranger, " tell me something I do not know.''

Carl felt his ire rising rapidly; the wealth which it was well known his father had amassed, had procured for him universal respect, and to be thus cavalierly addressed by a perfect stranger, much offended, whilst at the same time it amazed him. Yet the feeling which we have before described, restrained him from giving vent to his passion. Carl Wilstadt had read numbers of the romantic legends of his country ; this might be an inhabitant of the nether world, come upon earth for the purpose of assisting him in love; he had also read the Arabian Nights' Entertainments, and with the recollection of the disguises of the Caliph Haroun Alraschid full in his memory, he doubted whether the being before him was not some prince in disguise; nay, it might be even the emperor himself. Should any of these conjectures be right, the subject of them was highly calculated to forward his half-formed plans, and influenced by these considerations, he changed his intended tone of defiance into one of courtesy, and replied :

" On what subject would you wish to be enlightened, Mein Herr ?''

" What was you thinking of the instant before you saw me ?'' inquired he of the Sable Cloak, who had been engaged in attentively regarding his changing features.

Carl started, and fixing his eyes upon those of the

stranger, attempted to dive into his meaning. From his glance, however, he learned nothing; the bright eyes which met his gaze confused him, and he bent his looks on the ground. He must, he supposed, have given utterance to some thoughtless expression, which had reached the ears of Sable Cloak, and excited his curiosity; and yet he did not recollect allowing a single word to pass his lips. The pause which ensued was broke by the stranger, rejoining—

" Tell me something of Caroline Hernsdorff!"

The surprise with which Carl had regarded his new acquaintance, was now lost in anger; he little doubted but that his actions had been watched, and that this was the person to whom Caroline was betrothed. He rose in a stately manner from his recumbent position, and proudly said—

" Ere I answer thy questions, impertinent evesdropper, tell me thy name."

The owner of the Sable Cloak laughed outright, and yet in the politest manner possible :—

" My name, good Carl, that is of trifling import; suffice it that I have a personal regard for you, and will assist the plans on which you are meditating. Nay, do not start; I know the whole secret of your love for Caroline Hernsdorff; in fact I was present at the interview in the garden."

" The deuce you was!" exclaimed Carl, giving way to a burst of unbounded amazement, and gazing on the speaker with outstretched eyes.

" Yes I was; and, as I said before, feeling an interest in your future happiness (Carl bowed), and perc eeiving that you would never summon sufficient resolution to make a formal declaration of love, I pushed the miniature from her hold, and thus revealed her love for you. Without my assistance you never can secure your mistress. Will you accept of my proffered aid?"

With faltering tongue, Carl inquired how he should repay his services.

" Of that anon," was the reply.

" How shall I be assured that you have the power, as well as the will to assist me? Your story of the miniature sounds well, but that may be framed to mock my credulity."

Again the unknown laughed—" Mock thy credulity! weak mortal! what interest thinkest thou I could have in mocking thy credulity? Listen to me: you wish to see her; without my assistance that is impossible. The shades of night are already thick around; Caroline is in her chamber, engaged so deeply in devotion, that no puny efforts of thine can distract her thoughts. Say but the word, and I will insure some moments to converse."

Carl felt assured that by refusing this help he should be acting aright; but after a short consideration, he acted as half mankind would have done—he accepted it.

A short time employed in brisk walking, brought them to the confines of the forest, and a short time farther, found them a few paces distant from what Carl well knew to be the window of Caroline's room. It was furnished with curtains, which were now tightly drawn, although a light within informed our student that the fair inmate had not yet sought repose.

The very last beam of day yet lingered in the west of a summer horizon, and attempted vainly to contend with the already powerful rays of a brightly-rising moon. The beauty of the surrounding scene was, however, lost upon our student, who stood gazing on the envious curtains which concealed from his sight the form of his beloved. The silence was broken by his companion :—

. " Go," he said, and his words sounded scornfully ; " go, endeavour to gain an interview; if you do not succeed, return to me, I will await you here."

Carl advanced, and with the utmost caution, attempted to render his near vicinity known to Caroline: he sang parts of duets which they had practised together, then he softly murmured her name, and when all these efforts had failed, he threw a handful of turf and stones against the window, but even this proved vain, and Carl returned discontented to he of the Sable Cloak.

" I will not," said the latter calmly, and without surprise, " inquire the success of your mission ; I am well aware of its failure; now go once more, and when you arrive under the window, she whom you wish to behold will appear."

With many forebodings, Carl turned from his new patron.

" St. Joachim defend me ! if I am dealing with the evil one ;" he muttered, and another second brought him under the window. For several minutes did he wait her promised appearance, but she came not ; and now convinced that he had been duped, he returned full of ire to the stranger. Ere he could speak, his usual scornful laugh burst from the latter, as he demanded, " What didst thou mutter as thou left me ? Fool! call not on saints to aid my spells. Away! and seek once more yonder window."

Carl obeyed, somewhat awed by the manner of the speaker : scarce had he reached it, when it was thrown open, and Caroline stepped out upon the balcony.

" Dearest," he softly whispered, " dearest Caroline."

A half scream escaped her lips, as she bent her eyes on the spot where her lover stood. "Oh, Carl," she answered, " my father has just informed me, that he to whom I am betrothed will be here to-morrow ; and he bid me prepare for an almost immediate marriage. Alas! alas! I fear all hope of escape is vain."

" Not so," answered Carl, and he saw that this fresh obstacle rendered instant action highly necessary; "not so: fly with me to some distant country, where no avaricious parents may appear to interrupt our happiness, let me——"

" Hush, hush," and she interrupted him with alarm, " I hear my father's step; away, oh haste away ; if he should find you here, I tremble at the idea of his rage."

" Not, I swear by heaven, not till you have promised to meet me."

" Well, I will be in the garden at noon to-morrow, but do not come if my father is in sight; he suspects our attachment, and——oh, go away." She darted in, and the window was closed.

Carl turned upon the villa with many mingled feelings, joy certainly was uppermost. Caroline had heard his proposal of flight without starting. True, blushes mantled on her cheek, but that was not against his cause. There certainly were divers unpleasant thoughts relative to future subsistence, should their parents prove inexorable; "but then," said Carl, "I can work, and with Caroline as my reward, I would work double, and support her in affluence." Poor Carl! what mistaken ideas were his!

So engaged had he been in meditation, that he looked not for the being by whose assistance he had gained the interview, and reached his little chamber, just as the gates of the college were about to be closed. The sight of his studies, which had this day been so completely neglected, gave him a momentary pang, but he stifled the unpleasant feeling, and throwing himself on his couch, he sought a transient repose.

Carl rose with the lark, and a few hours intense study served not only to repair the loss of the previous day, but to while away the tedious time which intervened between the hour of sunrise and the period which Caroline had fixed for their meeting. The sun shone sprightly, and Carl willingly hailed this as a favourable omen.

While yet deeply engaged, a low tap at the door surprized him, it opened immediately afterwards, and the gentleman in the Sable Cloak entered. With a calm smile and courteous bow he advanced to the table, first carefully closing the door, and then drawing to him the only stool which decorated the apartment, save that occupied by the student, he seated himself exactly opposite to the amazed Carl.

" You inquired on what terms I would render you my

aid, to obtain the object of your wishes, I am now come prepared to inform you.''

"Spare yourself the trouble, Mein Herr, I have resolved not to accept it," replied Carl, who yet retained a lively recollection of his new friend's imperative manner on the preceding evening.

"Indeed!" uttered calmly and with very little surprise; you fancy you can succeed without receiving help: you are wrong; a fresh and most unfortunate obstacle, which you little expect, has arisen, and which renders success without my assistance, impossible; and moreover, you have already received some services from me, for which, however, I do not demand any return.''

Carl was perfectly well aware, that it was indeed next to impossible to succeed without great assistance, and in fact, his sudden refusal arose more from an impetuous feeling of suppressed rage, than a fixed determination to decline his offers. Thus, after a short period, somewhat soothed by the polite tone of his visitor, he inquired—

"What do you propose to secure to me, and what must I do in return?"

He in the Sable Cloak drew from under his disguise a bundle of papers, folded carefully, and tied with red tape, not unlike the law papers of merry England. One of these was a shrivelled parchment, and this he unfolded and carefully read over. Having finished, he looked up, and said—

"I can promise you a life of half a century, a fortune immense, and Caroline Hernsdorff for a bride. In return for which I shall expect that, at the expiration of the stated time, you will become my slave for ever.''

"Ah! now I know thee, fiend! Hence!"

"Softly, softly; you then consent to resign Caroline to the arms of another? Well, be it so: I am content." He rose from his seat, tied up his papers, and prepared to depart. Carl paced the room in agony.

"Do you mean to keep your appointment with Caroline?"

"Assuredly," replied Carl, in a voice shaken with emotion.

"Of what use will that be? I tell thee it is useless unless thou wilt accept of my terms: in truth it will be impossible to obtain an interview again without my assistance, and as I do nothing precipitately, suppose I procure this meeting while you deliberate on my proposal. Hark! those chimes announce the hour of noon. Shall we be gone?"

Carl gave a tacit assent, and followed his conductor through the town towards the villa of Mein Herr Hernsdorff.

Numberless ideas flitted across his brain: "If," he thought, "I can persuade her to fly with me from Germany, I shall not need the assistance of him who walks by my side; and should I fail, sooner would I resign all hopes of happiness than agree to his proposal. Nevertheless, I will accept of his help in regard to this interview; it will bind me by no ties save that of gratitude; and gratitude, thank heaven, is no legal obligation."

While thus deeply engaged in thought, the eye of his companion was fixed intently upon him; and when at length his determination seemed fixed, a bitter smile played upon his lips.

"Observe," said Carl, actuated by the motives which we have detailed, "that though I accept of your service in this slight particular, no promise has escaped my lips."

His companion nodded: and without another word they reached the garden of the villa. Carl went to the same part of the wall which he had scaled the preceding day, and was about to spring over, when his arm was held by his companion.

"Stop," he exclaimed,—"Master Hernsdorff, fearful of robbers, has set spring guns upon this part of his grounds; had you advanced another step, a bullet would have apprized you of this fact: follow me, I will conduct you to a place from whence you may gain the garden."

He led the way to a different part, where the high wall was hid from the view of those walking inside by a row of fine trees, while a similar number flourished on the exterior. He in the Sable Cloak pointed out one, the trunk of which was rugged and gnarled: this it was perfectly easy to ascend, and another minute beheld Carl on the top of the wall, from whence the eye could command a view of the whole of the garden. The stranger followed him with equal celerity, and they both surveyed the garden with apparently equal interest. In one of the walks they discovered Mein Herr, walking with his daughter leaning on his arm.

Scarce could Carl believe that the girl he now beheld

was the very identical one from whom he had parted in sorrow the preceding evening. Her step was light and elastic, her eyes bright and gay, her cheeks glowing with delight. She was listening attentively to the words of her father, who appeared enforcing some measure which did not meet with her entire approbation, although the prevailing sentiment in her bosom was evidently ecstatic joy.

"They are talking of her intended husband," said the stranger; "and she receives the information he gives with transport."

"Liar!" shouted Carl, agitated now by a new and most powerful feeling, that of jealousy, and totally forgetful of his concealed situation. A distant sound most probably reached the ears of the father and daughter, as they both turned to the spot where Carl stood, but not seeing any object, their regards were again turned away, and their walk resumed.

The Sable Cloak smiled with his usual contempt.

"Fools fight about the epithet you have applied to me; I am more prudent, and shall find ample revenge in discovering to you the truth of what I have asserted. I promised to procure you an interview, thus do I perform my engagement."

He waved his hand, and a domestic was seen advancing from the house; he approached Mein Herr, and appeared to inform him that his presence was required. Her father once more enforced most emphatically, as he seemed by his gestures, her compliance with some command, to which she now acceded: he followed the servant to the house, and Caroline pursued her walk.

With agility Carl descended a tree on the inner side, and approached her, although not without feeling some degree of agitation.

Carelessly strolling on, her eyes chanced to rest on the form of her advancing lover; and she hastened to meet him.

" Oh! Carl, I have seen him!"

" Seen! seen who?"

" Why, my intended husband, and he is so handsome, and so amiable; and Carl, my father says I shall never marry any one but him, and I should not like to act against his positive commands: indeed I like him as well as I do you; an so—" she paused, looking somewhat confused.

" Do I hear rightly?" exclaimed the wretched Carl: " oh! merciful heaven! anything but this could I have borne. Caroline! had you still loved me, had you not proved thus fickle and inconstant, not all the world should have parted us; I could have died to secure your happiness—but this is so unexpected— so," his voice faltered—and rushing from her, he again ascended the tree, and left the garden.

The sight of his agony excited the most painful feelings in the breast of Caroline; scalding tears filled her eyes, and " Carl, Carl, dearest Carl!" burst from her lips: he was beyond hearing; another moment, and she saw him franticly bound over the wall from her sight. She entered the bower, and threw herself despondingly on the seat; " I have wounded the heart which loved me. Oh, wretched Caroline! what demon could influence thee? Oh, why did I acceed to the wishes of my father?" Fresh tears flowed at every word, and she experienced the severest pang which our bosoms are capable of feeling, the sting of self-reproach. Could Carl have beheld her at that moment, even he must have owned himself amply revenged.

A short time beheld Carl once more in his chamber; "she is not worthy of being remembered," he cried, and he thought of nothing but her.

"I will draw," he exclaimed; but his pencil did nought but trace the features of his faithless love.

"I will compose," but his pen merely stained the spotless paper with the name of "Caroline Hernsdorff." In despair, his pen was thrown away, and leaning his head on the table, a burst of tears somewhat soothed his agonized feelings.

Several hours past: he was sitting on a stool, his arms crossed on his breast, his face pale as marble, his eyes fixed intently on vacancy, when a low tap at his door announced a visitor. Carl spoke not, in fact he heard it not: one sole thought, one fixed idea, bound up his faculties, and rendered all outward objects as nothing. A second tap, and then the door opened, and having given admittance to the form of some visitor, again closed. Still moved he not, until the idea burst upon his brain that the attentive regards of some being on the opposite side of the table, were fixed on him. He started from his lethargy, and beheld the form of his tormentor. A most powerful emotion of rage seized him: he rushed to the place where a rusty sword decorated the wall, and snatching it down, attempted to disengage it from its sheath; his eyes fixed on his visitor, glowing with rage. All these ominous preparations the stranger beheld with evident surprise.

" What is the matter, master student? What wouldst thou do?"

" I will destroy thee, monster!" madly replied the infuriated Carl; " I will rid the world of one cursed enchanter." With all his efforts, however, the rusty sword refused to leave its ancient friend and ally the scabbard, while his ears were tortured, and his feelings of anger augmented, by the loud peals of laughter with which his visitor saluted his many efforts. At length his perseverance was rewarded, and with furious gesture he rushed upon his enemy.

" Are you frantic?" shouted the latter, as he seized the arm of Carl, shook the sword from his hand, and sent him reeling to the side of the apartment; " what mad idea can induce you to behave thus to him whose object is to befriend you?"

" I want not your friendship," gasped the wretched Carl : " by spells and charms, you have estranged from me, the heart of her I loved ; you have bestowed on me with peculiar friendship, misery for life; and would now insult me; away! else will I summon my father confessor, and he shall exorcise the house."

He whom Carl addressed smiled with his usual scorn :——

" Your threat I despise; your charge I disown ; no spells have I used, save those in your favour. I came not here to insult you, but to require your definite answer respecting my proposal of this morning."

" Thou art a lying prophet; thou didst promise me

the love and the hand of Caroline, and she despises
me."

"To me that is nothing; sign my parchment," and
he produced it, "and I again promise thee her most
fervent love; nay more, I can promise thee her hand
shall be thine, ere four more suns have rose and set."

A pause ensued.

"I never will sign that parchment—no, I will not
comply——"

"You will then calmly resign Caroline Hernsdorff to
her betrothed husband, and yet say that you loved her?
thou art a most ardent lover, truly."

While the tempter yet spoke, a distant foot sounded
on the spiral stair-case, which led from the court-yard
to the chamber.

"Hearest thou that, Carl Wilstadt? it is the foot
of thy father; he has just arrived from Hamburgh, and
has brought with him thy intended bride, whose riches
are her principal attraction; be wise, while it is yet in
thy power."

He drew a seat to the table, opened the parchment,
dipped a pen in the inkstand and held it towards Carl,
whose convulsed features sufficiently evidenced the
frightful and conflicting emotions which raged within
his bosom. The foot drew near and yet nearer.

"Carl Wilstadt, the moment that your father enters
the room, I hasten away, never to return; this is the
last opportunity thou hast of being happy."

"Say again, what is it thou offerest?" eagerly, yet
shudderingly.

"Sign this, and I will give thee a long life; an

immense, and almost boundless store of wealth in thy coffers, and Caroline Hernsdorff in thy arms——Quick!''

The step sounded on the very threshold, Carl seized the pen, his heart throbbed violently, his hand trembled, he could not write; a moment passed, and he became sensible of his dangerous situation; the pen was flung aside.——

" Fiend, I defy thee, away, away !''

A smile of deadly enmity, and of disappointed malice, played on the lips of he in the Sable Cloak; he seized the parchment, and ere the door was wholly unclosed, was invisible to human ken.   The stool on which he had sat became suddenly vacant, and ere Carl could rouse from his astonishment, he was caught in the arms of his father.

The first congratulations over, Mien Herr Wilstadt, observing the paleness of his son, remarked :——

" I fear, my dear boy, that you have attended too closely to your studies; I have, however, arranged affairs for your immediate removal, and indeed Carl, also for your marriage.   I have selected a lady for you, with whom I am convinced you will be well pleased, and she now waits our arrival at the hotel.''

*   *   *   *   *

When arrived at the hotel, Carl was left for a few moments alone; at length two persons entered the apartment——one was the foot of his father, the other the light one of a female.——They came nearer——" Now Carl,'' and the voice sounded close to his ear, " welcome your fair bride !''

He turned, and perceived his father supporting the

form of a young girl, closely veiled: she trembled violently, and clung to his arm.

"Poor girl!" sighed Carl, mentally, and he took her small white hand and kissed it; "perchance the victim of parental avarice: well, if so, my whole life shall be spent in attempting to render thee happy, although the phanton, felicity, hath eluded my grasp for ever."

"Foolish youth," cried Mein Herr, "why stand kissing her hand, when two of the finest lips in the world are before you?"

As he spoke, he threw back her veil, and disclosed a countenance of bewitching beauty. "Now Carl, take her to your heart."

Carl was an obedient son, and consequently did as he was bid, although it must be confessed that his kisses appeared far more willing than forced,—it was his Caroline!

*　　*　　*　　*　　*

Happiness blest their union, and the narrow escape of Carl from the deep-laid snares of he in the Sable Cloak, afforded conversation for many a succeeding winter evening.

NICOLAS PEDROSA, THE BARBER OF MADRID.

NICOLAS PEDROSA, a busy little being, who followed the trades of shaver, surgeon, and man-midwife, in the town of Madrid, mounted his mule at the door of his shop in the Plazuela de los Affligidos, and pushed through the gate of San Bernardino, being called to a patient in the neighbouring village of Foncarral, upon a pressing occasion. Everybody knows that the ladies in Spain, in certain cases, do not give long warning to practitioners of a certain description, and nobody knew it better than Nicolas, who was resolved not to lose an inch of his way, nor of his mule's best speed by the way, if cudgelling could beat it out of her. It was plain to Nicolas's conviction, as plain could be, that his road laid straight forward to the little convent in front; the mule was of opinion, that the turning on the left, down the hill towards the Prado, was the road of all roads most familiar and agreeable to herself, and accordingly began to dispute the point of topography with Nicolas, by fixing her fore-feet resolutely in the ground, dipping her head at the same time between them, and launching heels and crupper furiously into the air in the way of argument. Little Pedrosa, who was armed at heel with one massy silver spur, of stout though ancient workmanship, resolutely applied the rusty rowel to the shoulder of his beast, driving it with all the good-will in the world to the very butt; and at the same time adroitly tucking his blue cloth capa under his right arm, and flinging the skirt over the left- shoulder *en cavalier*, began to lay about him with a stout ashen sapling upon the ears, pole, and cheeks of the recreant mule.   The fire now flashed from a pair of Andalusian eyes, as black as charcoal and not less inflammable, and taking the segara from his mouth, with which he had vainly hoped to have regaled his nostrils, in a sharp winter's evening, by the way, raised such a thundering troop of angels, saints, and martyrs, from St. Michael downwards, not forgetting his own name-sake, Saint Nicolas de Tolentino, by the way, that if curses could have made the mule to go, the dispute would have been soon ended; but not a saint could make her stir any other ways than upwards and down-wards at a stand.   A small troop of mendicant friars were at this moment conducting the host of a dying man.—' Nicolas Pedrosa,' says an' old friar, ' be pa-tient with your beast and spare your blasphemies: re-member Balaam.'—' Ah, Father,' replied Pedrosa, ' Balaam cudgelled his beast till she ·spoke, so will I mine till she roars.'—' Fie, fie, profane fellow,' cries another of the fraternity.—' Go about your work, friend,' quoth Nicolas, ' and let me go about mine : I warrant it is the more pressing of the two ; your pa-tient is going out of the world, mine- is coming into it.'—' Hear him,' cries a third, ' hear the vile wretch, how he blasphemes the body of God,'—and then the troop past slowly on to the tinkling of the bell.

A man must know nothing of a mule's ears who
does not know what a passion they have for the tinkling of a bell, and no sooner had the jingling chords
vibrated in the sympathetic organs of Pedrosa's beast,
than bolting forward with a sudden spring she ran
roaring into the throng of friars, trampling on some
and shouldering others at a most profane rate; when
Nicolas, availing himself of the impetus, and perhaps
not able to controul it, broke away, and was out of
sight in a moment. 'All the devils in hell blow fire
into thy tail, thou beast of Babylon,' muttered Nicolas
to himself, as he scampered along, never once looking
behind him, or stopping to apologize for the mischief
he had done to the bare feet and shirtless ribs of the
holy brotherhood.

Whether Nicolas saved his distance, as likewise, if
he did, whether it was a male or female Castilian he
ushered into the world, we shall not just now enquire,
contented to await his return in the first of the morning next day, when he had no sooner dismounted at
his shop, and delivered his mule to a sturdy Arragon-
ese wench, than Don Ignacio de Santos Aparacio,
alguazil mayor of the supreme and general inquisition,
put an order into his hand, signed and sealed by the
inquisitor-general, for the conveying his body to the
Casa, whose formidable door presents itself into the
street adjoining to the square in which Nicolas's brazen
basin hung forth the emblem of his trade.

The poor little fellow, trembling in every joint, and
with a face as yellow as saffron, dropt a knee to the
altar, which fronts the entrance, and crossed himself

most devoutly ; as soon as he had ascended the first
flight of stairs, a porter habited in black opened the
tremendous barricade, and Nicolas with horror heard
the grating of the heavy bolts that shut him in. He
was led through passages and vaults and melancholy
cells, till he was delivered into the dungeon, where he
was finally left to his solitary meditations. Hapless
being ! what a scene of horror. Nicolas felt all the
terrors of his condition, but being an Andalusian, and,
like his countrymen, of a lively imagination, he began
to turn over all the resources of his invention for some
happy fetch, if any such might occur, for helping him
out of the dismal limbo he was in : he was not long to
seek for the cause of his misfortune : his adventure
with the barefooted friars was a ready solution of all
difficulties of that nature, had there been any; there
was, however, another thing, which might have troubled a stouter heart than Nicolas's—he was a Jew.
This of a certain would have been a staggering item
in a poor devil's confession, but then it was a secret to
all the world but Nicolas, and Nicolas's conscience did
not just then urge him to reveal it ; he now began to
overhaul the inventory of his personals about him, and
with some satisfaction counted three little medals of
the Blessed Virgin, two Agnus Dei's, a Saint Nicolas
de Tolentino, and a formidable string of beads all
pendant from his neck and within his shirt; in his
pockets he had a paper of dried figs, a small bundle
of segars, a case of lancets, squirt, and forceps, and
two old razors in a leathern envelope ; these he had
delivered one by one to the alguazil, who first arrested

him,—' and let him make the most of them,' said he
to himself, ' they can never prove me an Israelite by a
case of razors.'—Upon a closer rummage, however, he
discovered in a secret pocket a letter, which the alguazil
had overlooked, and which his patient Donna Leonora
de Casafonda, had given him in charge to deliver as
directed. ' Well, well,' cried he, ' let it pass; there
can be no mystery in this harmless scrawl; a letter of
advice to some friend or relation, I'll not break the
seal; let the fathers read it, if they like, 'twill prove
the truth of my deposition, and help out my excuse for
the hurry of my errand, and the unfortunate adventure of my refractory mule.'—And now no sooner had
the recollection of the wayward mule crossed the brain
of poor Nicolas Pedrosa, than he began to blast her at
a furious rate. ' The scratches and the scab to boot
confound thy scurvy hide,' quoth he, ' thou ass-begot-
ten bastard whom Noah never let into his ark ! The
vengeance take thee for an uncreated barren beast of
promiscuous generation ! What devil's crotchet got
into thy capricious noddle, that thou shouldst fall in
love with that Nazaritish bell, and run bellowing like
Lucifer into the midst of those barefooted vermin,
who are more malicious and more greedy than the
locusts of Egypt ? Oh ! that I had the art of Simon
Magus, to conjure thee into this dungeon in my stead;
but I warrant thou art chewing thy barley straw without any pity for thy wretched master, whom thy jade's
tricks have delivered bodily to the tormentors, to be
the sport of these uncircumcised sons of Dagon.' And
now the cell door opened, when a savage figure en-

tered, carrying a huge parcel of clanking fetters, with a collar of iron, which he put round the neck of poor Pedrosa, telling him, with a truly diabolic grin, whilst he was rivetting it on, that it was a proper cravat for the throat of a blasphemer.—' Jesu-Maria,' quoth Pedrosa, ' is all this fallen upon me for only cudgelling a restive mule?'—' Ay,' cried the demon, ' and this is only a taste of what is to come,' at the same time slipping his pincers from the screw he was forcing to the head, he caught a piece of flesh in the forceps and wrenched it out of his cheek, laughing at poor Nicolas, whilst he roared aloud with the pain, telling him it was a just reward for the torture he had put him to awhile ago, when he tugged at a tooth till he broke it in his jaw. ' Ah, for the love of heaven,' cried Pedrosa, ' have more pity on me; for the sake of Saint Nicolas de Tolentino, my holy patron, be not so unmerciful to a poor barber-surgeon, and I will shave your worship's beard for nothing as long as I have life. One of the messengers of the auditory now came in, and bade the fellow strike off the prisoner's fetters, for that the holy fathers were in council and demanded him for examination. ' This is something extraordinary,' quoth the tormentor, ' I should not have expected it this twelvemonth to come.' Pedrosa's fetters were struck off; some brandy was applied to staunch the bleeding of his cheeks; his hands and face were washed, and a short jacket of coarse ticking thrown over him, and the messenger, with an assistant, taking him each under an arm, led him into a spacious chamber, where, at the head of a long table, sate his excellency the inquisitor-general, with six of his accessors, three on each side the chair of state : the alguazil mayor, a secretary, and two notaries, with other officers of the holy council, were attending in their places.

The prisoner was placed behind a bar at the foot of the table, between the messengers who brought him in; and having made his obeisance to the awful presence in the most supplicating manner, he was called upon, according to the usual form of questions, by one of the junior judges, to declare his name, parentage, profession, age, place of abode, and to answer various interrogatories of the like trifling nature : his excellency the inquisitor-general now opened his reverend lips, and in a solemn tone of voice, that penetrated to the heart of the poor trembling prisoner, interrogated him as follows :—

' Nicolas Pedrosa, we have listened to the account you give of yourself, your business, and connections ; now tell us for what offence, or offences, you are here standing a prisoner before us : examine your own heart, and speak the truth from your conscience without prevarication or disguise.'—' May it please your excellency,' replied Pedrosa, ' with all due submission to your holiness and this reverend assembly, my most equitable judges, I conceive I stand here before you for no worse a crime than that of cudgelling a refractory mule; an animal so restive in its nature, under correction of your holiness be it spoken, that although I were blest with the forbearance of holy Job, for like him too I am married, and my patience hath been exercised by a wife, yet could I not forbear to smite my beast for her obstinacy, and the rather because I was summoned in the way of my profession, as I have already made known to your most merciful ears, upon a certain crying occasion, which would not admit of a moment's delay.'

'Recollect yourself, Nicolas,' said his excellency the inquisitor-general, 'was there nothing else you did, save smiting your beast?'

'I take Saint Nicolas de Tolentino to witness,' replied he, 'that I know of no other crime, for which I can be responsible at this righteous tribunal, save smiting my unruly beast.'

'Take notice, brethren,' exclaimed the inquisitor, 'this unholy wretch holds trampling over friars to be no crime.'

'Pardon me, holy father,' replied Nicolas, 'I hold it for the worst of crimes, and therefore willingly surrender my refractory mule to be dealt with as you see fit, and if you impale her alive, it will not be more than she deserves.'

'Your wits are too nimble, Nicolas,' cried the judge; 'have a care they do not run away with your discretion: recollect the blasphemies you uttered in the hearing of those pious people.'

'I humbly pray your excellency,' answered the prisoner, 'to recollect that anger is a short madness, and I hope allowances will be made by your holy council for words spoken in haste to a rebellious mule: the prophet Balaam was thrown off his guard with a simple ass, and what is an ass compared to a mule: if your excellency had seen the lovely creature that was screaming in agony till I came to her relief, and how fine a boy I ushered into the world, which would have been lost but for my assistance, I am sure I should not be condemned for a few hasty words spoke in passion.'

' Sirrah !' cried one of the puisne judges, ' respect the decency of the court.'

' Produce the contents of this fellow's pockets before the court,' said the president ; ' lay them on the table.'

' Monster,' resumed the aforesaid puisne judge, taking up the forceps, ' what is the use of this diabolical machine ?'

' Unnatural wretch ! you have murdered the mother.'

' The mother of God forbid !' exclaimed Pedrosa, ' I believe I have a proof in my pocket, that will acquit me of that charge ; and so saying, he tendered the letter we have before made mention of: the secretary took it, and, by command of the court, read as follows :

' Senor Don Manuel de Herrera.

' When this letter, which I send by Nicolas Pedrosa, shall reach your hands, you shall know that I am safely delivered of a lovely boy after a dangerous labour, in consideration of which I pray you to pay to the said Nicolas Pedrosa the sum of twenty gold pistoles, which sum his excellency—'

' Hold !' cried the inquisitor-general, starting hastily from his seat, and snatching away the letter, 'there is more in this than meets the eye: break up the court; I must take an examination of this prisoner in private.'

As soon as the room was cleared, the inquisitor-general, beckoning to the prisoner to follow him, retired into a private closet, where, throwing himself carelessly into an arm chair, he turned a gracious countenance upon the poor affrighted accoucheur, and bidding him sit down upon a low stool by his side, thus accosted him :—' Take heart, senor Pedrosa, your imprisonment is not likely to be very tedious, for I have a commission you must execute without loss of time: you have too much consideration for yourself to betray a trust, the violation of which must involve you in inevitable ruin, and can in no degree attaint my character, which is far enough beyond the reach of malice: be attentive, therefore, to my orders; execute them punctually, and keep my secret as you tender your own life: dost thou know the name and condition of the lady whom thou hast delivered?' Nicolas assured him he did not, and his excellency proceeded as follows :— ' Then I tell thee, Nicolas, it is the illustrious Donna Leonora de Casafonda : her husband is the president of Quito, and daily expected with the next arrivals from the South Seas ; now, though measures have been taken for detaining him at the port wherever he shall land, till he shall receive further orders, yet you must be sensible Donna Leonora's situation is somewhat delicate : it will be your business to take the speediest measures for her recovery; but as it seems she has had a dangerous and painful labour, this may be a work of more time than could be wished, unless some medicines more efficacious than common are administered: art thou acquainted with any such, friend Nicolas?'——' So please your excellency,' quoth Nicolas, 'my processes have been tolerably successful.'——' Thou talkest like a fool, friend Nicolas,' interrupting him, said the inquisitor; 'quick work must be wrought by quick medicines. Hast thou none such in thy botica? I'll answer for it thou hast not; therefore look you, sirrah, here is a little vial compounded by a famous chemist; see that you mix it in the next apozom you administer to Donna Leonora; it is the most capital sedative in nature; give her the whole of it, and let her husband return when he will, depend upon it he will make no discoveries from her.'——' Humph!' quoth Nicolas within himself, ' Well said, inquisitor!' He took the vial with all possible respect, and was not wanting in professions of the most inviolable fidelity and secrecy. ——' No more words, friend Nicolas,' quoth the inquisitor, ' upon that score; I do not believe thee one jot the more for all thy promises; my dependence is upon thy fears and not on thy faith; I fancy thou hast seen enough of this place not to be willing to return to it once for all.'——Having so said, he rang a bell, and ordered Nicolas to be forthwith liberated, bidding the messenger return his clothes instantly to him, with all that belonged to him, and having slipped a purse into his hand well filled with doubloons, he bade him begone about his business, and not to see his face again till he had executed his commands.

Nicolas bolted out of the porch without taking leave of the altar, and never checked his speed till he found himself fairly housed under shelter of his own beloved brass basin.——'Aha!' quoth Nicolas, 'my lord inquisitor, I see the king is not likely to gain a subject more by your intrigues : a pretty job you have set me about: and so, when I have put the poor lady to rest with your damned sedative, my tongue must be stopt next to prevent its babbling ; but I'll show you I was not born in Andalusia for nothing.' Nicolas now opened a secret drawer and took out a few pieces of money, which in fact was his whole stock of cash in the world ; he loaded and primed his pistols, and carefully lodged them in the housers of his saddle, he buckled to his side his trusty spada, and hastened to caparison his mule. ' Ah, thou imp of the old one,' quoth he as he entered the stable, 'art not ashamed to look me in the face ? But come, hussy, thou owest me a good turn methinks, stand by me this once, and be friends for ever ! thou art in good case, and if thou wilt put thy best foot foremost, like a faithful beast, thou shalt not want for barley by the way.' The bargain was soon struck between Nicolas and his mule, he mounted her in the happy moment, and pointing his course towards the bridge of Toledo, which proudly strides with half a dozen lofty arches over a stream scarce three feet wide, he found himself as completely in a desert in half a mile's riding, as if he had been dropped in the centre of Arabia Petræa. As Nicolas's journey was not a tour of curiosity, he did not amuse himself with a peep at Toledo, or Talavera, or even Merida, by the way ; for the same reason he took a *circumbendibus* round the frontier town of Badajoz, and crossing a little brook refreshed his mule with the last draught of Spanish water, and instantly congratulated himself upon entering the territory of Portugal. 'Bravo!' quoth he, patting the neck of his mule, 'thou shalt have a supper this night of the best sieve meat that Estramadura can furnish : we are now in a country where the scattered flock of Israel fold thick and fare well.' He now began to chaunt the Song of Solomon, and gently ambled on in the joy of his heart.

When Nicolas at length reached the city of Lisbon, he hugged himself in his good fortune ; still he recollected that the inquisition has long arms, and he was yet in a place of no perfect security. Our adventurer had in early life acted as assistant-surgeon in a Spanish frigate bound to Buenos Ayres, and being captured by a British man-of-war, and carried into Jamaica, had very quietly passed some years in that place as journeyman apothecary, in which time he had acquired a tolerable acquaintance with the English language ; no sooner then did he discover the British ensign flying on the poop of an English frigate then lying in the Tagus, than he eagerly caught the opportunity of paying a visit to the surgeon, and finding he was in want of a mate, offered himself, and was entered in that capacity for a cruise against the French and Spaniards, with whom Great Britain was then at war. In this secure asylum Nicolas enjoyed the first happy moments he had experienced for a long time past, and being a lively good-humoured little fellow, and one that touched the

guitar and sung sequidillas with a tolerable grace, he
soon recommended himself to his shipmates, and grew
in favour with every body on board, from the captain to
the cook's mate.

When they were out upon the cruise hovering on the
Spanish coast, it occurred to Nicolas that the inquisitor-
general of Madrid had told him of the expected arrival
of the president of Quito, and having imparted this to
one of the lieutenants, he reported it to the captain, and
as the intelligence seemed of importance, he availed
himself of it by hauling into the track of the homeward-
bound galleons, and great was the joy when, at the
break of the morning, the man at the mast-head announced a square-rigged vessel in view : the ardour of
a chace now set all hands at work, and a few hours
brought them near enough to discern that she was
a Spanish frigate, and seemingly from a long voyage :
little Pedrosa, as alert as the rest, stript himself for his
work, and repaired to his post in the cock-pit, whilst
the thunder of the guns rolled incessantly overhead ;
three cheers from the whole crew at length announced
the moment of victory, and a few more minutes ascer-
tained the good news that the prize was a frigate richly
laden from the South Seas, with the governor of Quito
and his suite on board.

Pedrosa was now called upon deck, and sent on board
the prize as interpreter to the first lieutenant, who was
to take possession of her.   He found everything in confusion, a deck covered with the slain, and the whole
crew in consternation at an event they were in no
degree prepared for, not having received any intimation

of a war. He found the officers in general, and the passengers without exception, under the most horrid impressions of the English, and expecting to be plundered, and perhaps butchered without mercy. Don Manuel de Casafonda the governor, whose countenance bespoke a constitution far gone in a decline, had thrown himself on a sofa in the last state of despair, and given way to an effusion of tears; when the lieutenant entered the cabin he rose trembling from his couch, and with the most supplicating action presented to him his sword, and with it a casket which he carried in his other hand; as he tendered these spoils to his conqueror, whether through weakness or of his own will, he made a motion of bending his knee: the generous Briton, shocked at the unmanly overture, caught him suddenly with both hands, and turning to Pedrosa, said aloud—'Convince this gentleman he is fallen into the hands of an honourable enemy.'—'Is it possible!' cried Don Manuel, and lifting up his streaming eyes to the countenance of the British officer, saw humanity, valour, and generous pity so strongly charactered in his youthful features, that the conviction was irresistible. 'Will he not accept my sword?' cried the Spaniard. 'He desires you to wear it, till he has the honour of presenting you to his captain.'—'Ah, then he has a captain,' exclaimed Don Manuel, 'his superior will be of another way of thinking; tell him this casket contains my jewels; they are valuable; let him present them as a lawful prize, which will enrich the captor; his superior will not hesitate to take them from me.'—'If they are your excellency's private property,' replied Pedrosa, 'I am

ordered to assure you, that if your ship was loaded
with jewels, no British officer, in the service of his
king, will take them at your hands; the ship and
effects of his Catholic Majesty are the only prize of the
captors; the personals of the passengers are inviolate.'
—'Generous nation!' exclaimed Don Manuel, 'how
greatly have I wronged thee !'—The boats of the British
frigate now came alongside, and part of the crew was
shifted out of the prize, taking their clothes and trunks
along with them, in which they were very cordially
assisted by their conquerors. The barge soon after
came aboard with an officer in the stern-sheets, and
the crew in their white shirts and velvet caps, to escort
the governor and the ship's captain on board the frigate, which lay with her sails to the mast awaiting
their arrival; the accommodation-ladder was slung
over the side, and manned for the prisoners, who were
received on the gang-way by the second lieutenant,
whilst perfect silence and the strictest discipline reigned
in the ship, where all were under the decks, and no
inquisitive curious eyes were suffered to wound the
feelings of the conquered even with a glance; in the
door of his cabin stood the captain, who received them
with that modest complaisance, which does not revolt
the unfortunate by an overstrained politeness; he was
a man of high birth and elegant manners, with a heart
as benevolent as it was brave: such an address, set off
with a person finely formed and perfectly engaging,
could not fail to impress the prisoners with the most
favourable ideas; and as Don Manuel spoke French
fluently, he could converse with the British captain

E

without the help of an interpreter. As he expressed
an impatient desire of being admitted to his parole,
that he might revisit friends and connections, from
which he had been long separated, he was overjoyed to
hear that the English ship would carry her prize into
Lisbon; and that he would there be set on shore, and
permitted to make the best of his way from thence to
Madrid; he talked of his wife with all the ardour of
the most impassioned lover, and apologized for his
tears, by imputing them to the agony of his mind, and
the infirmity of his health, under the dread of being
longer separated from an object so dear to his heart,
and on whom he doated with the fondest affection.
The generous captor indulged him in these conversa-
tions, and, being a husband himself, knew how to
allow for all the tenderness of his sensations. ' Ah,
sir,' cried Don Manuel, ' would to heaven it were in
my power to have the honour of presenting my beloved
Leonora to you on our landing at Lisbon. Perhaps,'
added he, turning to Pedrosa, who at that moment
entered the cabin, ' this gentleman, whom I take to be
a Spaniard, may have heard the name of Donna Leonora
de Casafonda; if he has been at Madrid, it is possible
he may have seen her; should that be the case, he can
testify to her external charms; I alone can witness to
the exquisite perfection of her mind.'—' Senor Don
Manuel,' replied Pedrosa, ' I have seen Donna Leonora,
and your excellency is warranted in all you can say in
her praise; she is of incomparable beauty.' These
words threw the uxorious Spaniard into raptures; his
eyes sparkled with delight; the blood rushed into his

emaciated cheeks, and every feature glowed with unutterable joy: he pressed Pedrosa with a variety of rapid inquiries, all which he evaded by pleading ignorance, saying that he only had a casual glance at her, as she passed along the Prado. The embarrassment, however, which accompanied these answers, did not escape the English captain, who shortly after drawing Pedrosa aside into the surgeon's cabin, was by him made acquainted with the melancholy situation of that unfortunate lady, and every particular of the story as before related: nay, the very vial was produced with its contents, as put into the hands of Pedrosa by the inquisitor.

'Can there be such villainy in man!' cried the British captain, when Pedrosa had concluded his detail: 'Alas! my heart bleeds for this unhappy husband: assuredly that monster has destroyed Leonora: as for thee, Pedrosa, whilst the British flag flies over thy head, neither Spain, nor Portugal, nor inquisitors, nor devils, shall annoy thee under its protection; but if thou ever venturest over the side of this ship, and rashly settest one foot upon catholic soil, when we arrive at Lisbon, thou art a lost man.'—'I were worse than a madman,' replied Nicolas, 'should I attempt it.'—'Keep close in this asylum then,' resumed the captain, 'and fear nothing. Had it been our fate to have been captured by the Spaniards, what would have become of thee?'—'In the worst of extremities,' replied Nicolas, 'I should have applied to the inquisitor's vial; but I confess I had no fears of that sort; a ship so commanded and so manned is in little danger of being carried into a Spanish port.'

——' I hope not,' said the captain, ' and I promise thee
thou shalt take thy chance in her, so long as she is
afloat under my command, and if we live to conduct
her to England, thou shalt have thy proper share of
prize-money, which, if the galleon breaks up according
to her entries, will be something towards enabling thee
to shift, and if thou art as diligent in thy duty, as I am
persuaded thou wilt be, whilst I live thou shalt never
want a seaman's friend.'——At these cheering words, little
Nicolas threw himself at the feet of his generous preserver, and with streaming eyes poured out his thanks
from a heart animated with joy and gratitude.——The
captain raising him by the hand, forbade him, as he
prized his friendship, ever to address him in that posture any more: ' Thank me, if you will,' added he,
' but thank me as one man should another; let no knees
bend in this ship but to the name of God.——But now,'
continued he, ' let us turn our thoughts to the situation
of our unhappy Casafonda: we are now drawing near
to Lisbon, where he will look to be liberated on his
parole.'——' By no means let him venture into Spain,'
said Pedrosa; ' I am well assured there are orders to
arrest him in every port or frontier town, where he may
present himself.'——' I can well believe it,' replied the
captain. ' This piteous case will require further deli-
beration; in the mean time let nothing transpire on
your part, and keep yourself out of his sight as carefully as you can.'——This said, the captain left the cabin,
and both parties repaired to their several occupations.

As soon as the frigate and her prize cast anchor in
the Tagus, Don Manuel de Casafonda impatiently re-

minded our captain of his promised parole. The painful moment was now come, when an explanation of some sort became unavoidable. The generous Englishman, with a countenance expressive of the tenderest pity, took the Spaniard's hand in his, and seating him on a couch beside him, ordered the centinel to keep the cabin private, and delivered himself as follows:

'Senor Don Manuel, I must now impart to you an anxiety which I labour under on your account ; I have strong reason to suspect you have enemies in your own country, who are upon the watch to arrest you on your landing: when I have told you this, I expect you will repose such trust in my honour, and the sincerity of my regard for you, as not to demand a further explanation of the particulars on which my intelligence is founded.'

'Heaven and earth !' cried the astonished Spaniard, 'who can be those enemies I have to fear, and what can I have done to deserve them?'—'So far I will open myself to you,' answered the captain, 'as to point out the principal to you, the inquisitor-general.'—'The best friend I have in Spain,' exclaimed the governor, 'my sworn protector, the patron of my fortune. He my enemy ? Impossible.'—'Well, sir,' replied the captain, 'if my advice does not meet belief, I must so far exert my authority for your sake, as to make this ship your prison till I have waited on our minister at Lisbon, and made the necessary inquiries for your safety ; suspend your judgment on the seeming harshness of this measure till I return to you again ;' and at the same time, rising from his seat, he gave orders for the barge, and leaving strict injunctions with the first lieutenant not to allow of the governor's quitting the frigate, he put off for the shore, and left the melancholy Spaniard buried in profound and silent meditation.

The emissaries of the inquisition having at last traced Pedrosa to Lisbon, and there gained intelligence of his having entered on board the frigate, our captain had no sooner turned into the porch of the hotel of Buenos Ayres, than he was accosted by a messenger of state, with a requisition from the prime minister's office for the surrender of one Nicolas Pedrosa, a subject of Spain, and a criminal, who had escaped out of the prison of the inquisition in Madrid, where he stood charged with high crimes and misdemeanours. As soon as this requisition was explained to our worthy captain, without condescending to a word in reply, he called for pen and ink, and writing a short order to the officer commanding on board, instantly dispatched the midshipman who attended him, to the barge, with directions to make the best of his way back to the frigate, and deliver it to the lieutenant. Then turning to the messenger, he said to him in a resolute tone—'That Spaniard is now borne on my books, and before you shall take him out of the service of my king, you must sink his ship.' Not waiting for a reply, he immediately proceeded without stopping to the house of the British minister at the further end of the city. Here he found Pedrosa's intelligence, with regard to the governor of Quito, expressly verified, for the order had come down even to Lisbon, upon the chance of the Spanish frigate's taking shelter in that port. To this minister he related the horrid tale which Pedrosa had delivered to him, and with his concurrence it was determined to forward letters into Spain, which Don Manuel should be advised to write to his lady and friends at Madrid, and to wait their answer before any further discoveries were imparted to him respecting the blacker circumstances of the case. In the mean time it was resolved to keep the prisoner safe in his asylum.

The generous captain lost no time in returning to his frigate, where he immediately imparted to Don Manuel the intelligence he had obtained at the British minister's. —' This indeed,' cried the afflicted Spaniard, ' is a stroke I was in no respect prepared for; I had fondly persuaded myself there was not in the whole empire of Spain a more friendly heart than that of the inquisitor's; to my beloved Leonora he had ever shown the tenderness of a paternal affection from her very childhood; by him our hands were joined; his lips pronounced the nuptial benediction, and through his favour I was promoted to my government. Grant, Heaven, no misfortune hath befallen my Leonora; surely she cannot have offended him, and forfeited his favour.'— 'As I know him not,' replied the captain, ' I can form no judgment of his motives; but this I know, that if a man's heart is capable of cruelty, the fittest school to learn it in must be the inquisition.' The proposal was now suggested of sending letters into Spain, and the governor retired to his desk for the purpose of writing them; in the afternoon of the same day the minister paid a visit to the captain, and receiving a packet from the hands of Don Manuel, promised to get it forwarded, by a safe conveyance, according to direction.

In due course of time this fatal letter from Leonora opened all the horrible transaction to the wretched husband:—

'The guilty hand of an expiring wife, under the agonizing operation of a mortal poison, traces these few trembling lines to an injured wretched husband. If thou hast any pity for my parting spirit fly the ruin that awaits thee, and avoid this scene of villainy and horror. When I tell thee I have borne a child to the monster whose poison runs in my veins, thou wilt abhor thy faithless Leonora: had I strength to relate to thee the subtle machinations which betrayed me to disgrace, thou wouldst pity and perhaps forgive me. Oh agony! can I write his name? The inquisitor is my murderer—My pen falls from my hand—Farewell for ever.'

Had a shot passed through the heart of Don Manuel, it could not more effectually have stopt its motions than the perusal of this fatal writing. He dropped lifeless on the couch, and but for the care and assistance of the captain and Pedrosa, in that posture he had probably expired. Grief like his will not be described by words, for to words it gave no utterance; 'twas suffocating, silent woe.

Let us drop the curtain over this melancholy pause in our narration, and attend upon the mournful widower now landed upon English ground, and conveyed by his humane and generous preserver to the house of a noble earl, the father of our amiable captain, and a man by his virtues still more conspicuous than by his rank. Here amidst the gentle solicitudes of a benevolent family, in one of the most enchanting spots on earth, in a climate most salubrious and restorative to a constitution exhausted by heat, and a heart nearly broken with sorrow, the reviving spirits of the unfortunate Don Manuel gave the first symptoms of a possible recovery. At the period of a few tranquillizing weeks here passed in the bosom of humanity, letters came to hand from the British minister at Lisbon, in answer to a memorial, that I should have stated to have been drawn up by the friendly captain before his departure from that port, with a detail of facts deposed and sworn to by Nicolas Pedrosa, which memorial, with the documents attached to it, was forwarded to the Spanish court by special express from the Portuguese premier. By these letters it appeared, that the high dignity of the person impeached by this statement of facts, had not been sufficient to screen him from a very serious and complete investigation : in the course of which facts had been so clearly brought home to him by the confession of his several agents, and the testimony of the deceased Leonora's attendants, together with her own written declarations, whilst the poison was in operation, that though no public sentence had been executed upon the criminal, it was generally understood he was either no longer in existence, or in a situation never to be heard of any more, till, roused by the awakening trump, he shall be summoned to his tremendous last account. As for the unhappy widower, it was fully signified to him from authority, that his return to Spain, whether upon exchange or parole, would be no longer opposed, nor had he any thing to apprehend on the part of government when he should there arrive. The same was signified in fewer words to the exculpated Pedrosa.

Whether Don Manuel de Casafonda will, in time to come, avail himself of these overtures, time alone can prove. As for Nicolas, whose prize-money has set him up in a comfortable little shop in Duke's-place, where he breathes the veins and cleanses the bowels of his Israelitish brethren, in a land of freedom and toleration, his merry heart is at rest, save only when, with fire in his eyes, and vengeance on his tougue, he anathematizes the inquisition; and struts into the synagogue every sabbath with as bold a step and as erect a look as if he was himself high priest of the temple, going to perform sacrifice upon the re-assembling of the scattered tribes.

THE ELOPEMENT; AN ITALIAN STORY.

The Cavalier Nimagri á Revescio, a descendant of a noble Venetian family, whose name it is immaterial to mention, more particularly as the fact happened only some fifty years ago, being on his way to Rome, passed through Caserta, and wanting a servant, his valet having been taken dangerously ill on the road, enquired of the host, where he alighted, whether he could recommend him such a one? The host said he would enquire, and towards the evening brought a man up, who he said wanted a place. The host having retired, the Cavalier Nimagri asked the man what he could do? To which Gasparo, the servant, answered, " Nothing, sir."— " Nothing," said the cavalier, " cannot you dress hair, shave, &c. ?"—" No, sir ; but have good will, and will learn anything."—" But what has been your employment ?"—" A very bad one," said Gasparo, " but I am heartily sick of it, and am determined to get my bread honestly and live in the fear of God."—" But what are you, where do you come from?"—" Oh, sir," he continued, " I am a Sicilian, Gasparo is my name ; take pity on a poor repentant sinner ! hitherto I have been only a thief and a murderer, who, for a ducat or two would have murdered any man." Don Nimagri was astonished at the singularity of the case, and not a little staggered at the horrible countenance before him, wherein his former trade was strikingly depicted, but being a young man of uncommon courage, and altogether struck with the candour and simplicity of the fellow's tale, as well as the unaffected repentance he showed, he hired him, and he has often been heard to say, in his life he never met with a more trusty or faithful servant.

The next day the cavalier pursued his intended journey to Rome; on the second evening, having stopped at one of the best inns at Mecerra, while Don Nimagri was at supper, the host came in, and apologizing for the intrusion, said, " Signor Cavalier, there is a very noble youth below, just arrived, who, upon hearing I had but one gentleman traveller in the house, has begged I would ask your excellency whether you would allow him the pleasure of your society: I assure you, sir," said the host, " he is a very handsome young man, and, I dare say, the son of some nobleman of the first rank, who has been playing some thoughtless pranks ; run away from college, or some such trick." Don Nimagri, who was naturally of a kind disposition, desired the host to give his compliments to the gentleman, and say, he should be very happy in his company. In a few minutes the host introduced the guest, a very elegant youth, seemingly about eighteen, whose genteel and prepossessing appearance bespoke him of high birth ; he was in stature rather short, delicate but well proportioned, of a fair complexion, with beautiful and animated eyes ; after the usual compliments on such occasions, an addition was ordered to the supper. Don Nimagri's curiosity was a good deal excited by the manners and conversation of his guest ; it was sensible, but reserved.

Don Nimagri was too well bred to pry into his guest's affairs, but there was a visible uneasiness about the youth that distressed him; he endeavoured to rouse him by every means in his power, but the stranger answered but little; scarcely eat anything; sighed deeply; and, upon the whole, seemed to be greatly agitated. Don Nimagri, however, imagining he might have some affair of honour on his hands, generously offered the stranger every assistance in his power. Supper being ended, the youth got up, paced awhile along the room, and, at last, addressing the cavalier, said in a hurried tone, 'Noble signor, I have a favour to ask you: will you allow me, if the host can accommodate us with a double-bedded room, to sleep in the same apartment?" Don Nimagri hesitated not an instant, but rang for the host, and enquired for a room with two beds; the host answered, that he was sorry to say he had no such thing in the inn. Don Nimagri perceiving the host's answer very much increased the youth's inquietude, though he could not rightly guess at the cause, said, '' Well, signor, we must do as well as we can; the night is very hot; for my part I only mean to take off my coat and boots, slip on my dressing gown, and lay on the bed, for I propose starting very early, and to travel in the cool of the morning;" and, as Gasparo came in to receive orders, he desired his horse to be ready by five o'clock. These matters being settled, they retired to rest.

Don Nimagri would have been glad to have had a few hours sleep, but our youth was so restless as he lay on the bed, that it seemed impossible. Sleep, how-

ever, had at last overpowered the signor cavaliero ; he
had scarcely slept two hours, when he was roused by
a tremendous noise, as if the whole inn was in arms ;
he listened, and the noise still increasing, he jumped
up ; scarcely was he on his feet, when a loud rap was
heard at the room door, and two voices demanded admittance.   The youth, at the sound of the voices, ran
to Don Nimagri, and hardly able to articulate a word,
caught hold of his arm and cried, " Oh, save me,
signor ! I am an unfortunate young *woman* !" and fell
at his feet.   The cavalier had not a moment to think,
for they threatened to break open the door ;   upon
which Don Nimagri called to them, and said if they
dared to force the door, without a proper order from
the magistrate, he would blow their brains out, and
that he was well prepared to encounter a host of them ;
to which they replied they had.   " If you have," said
the cavalier, " thrust it under the door, and if it is a
true one, I will open the door ;" but that was not the
case, they were not in possession of any such a thing.
After many useless threats, they said they would fetch
a police officer, and retired.
    Meanwhile Gasparo, on the first hearing of the bus-
tle, had equipped himself with two large pistols in his
belt, a poniard, a huge sword which he always wore,
and came in to his master ; what was to be done with
the lady was the first question ; the host was called,
and a purse of ducats put into his hand, (the best
pleaders for protection) ; the state of the case being
told him, he proposed, while they were gone to procure an order (which he had no doubt they would

obtain, as the magistrate of the place was by no means invulnerable against the attack of a full purse), that the lady should be hidden in the hay-loft under some trusses, properly arranged for the purpose. This being done, the cavalier threw himself carelessly on the bed, and waited in great anxiety to hear of the lady's safety, till Gasparo ran in, and cried out, " *Il Diavolo istesso non la troverebbe*,"—the devil himself could not find her out, she is so well concealed. It was but a short time after every thing was settled, that the two gentlemen returned accompanied by an officer, who was desired to thrust the warrant under the door, if he really had one. Don Nimagri finding that it was a magistrate's order, and knowing the lady was safe, ordered Gasparo to open the door; the strangers judging by the appearance of Don Nimagri, and Gasparo's terrible figure, that the one was a person of some consequence, and well protected, began to apologize, stating that they were in search of a sister who had run away from home to avoid an union with a nobleman of her father's choice, and whom they were determined to secure. They searched everywhere, and as one of the brothers was looking under the bed, Gasparo, who was perhaps seized with an itching after his old habits, was winking and blinking at his master, with a piteous imploring face, to let him have a pop or two at them; and it was with difficulty he was able, by threatening looks, and a grasp of his arm, to prevent him from discharging both his pieces. Being disappointed in their search, the three men withdrew.

As soon as Don Nimagri thought they were safe,

Gasparo and himself went to release the affrighted lady, who was more dead than alive; some refreshments being brought in, Donna Colomba, having recovered a little, related her story to her protector, informing him that her cruel father, for the sake of interest, insisted she should marry an old dotard, who was old enough to be her grandfather, and whose vices and character she abhorred. "But what do you intend to do?" said our young champion. "Signor," added she, with a bewitching grace, and tears glistening in her fine eyes, "I am under your protection; the interest you have shewn for my safety, repels every idea of fear in me, and I have no hesitation in entrusting my life and my honour in your hands, if you will but escort me with your servant as far as Benevento; I have, at a short distance from thence, an aunt, an abbess, under whose sacred care I shall be safe, and where I mean to take the veil: do but this, and I will ever be grateful to you."

Don Nimagri was too much of a man and a cavalier to withstand the entreaties of a distressed fair one; he immediately gave orders for a carriage to be got ready, desired Gasparo to saddle their horses, look to the pistols in both saddles, and be quick. Gasparo flew: the chaise being ready, and the host liberally paid, the better to seal his lips, Donna Colomba and Don Nimagri leaped into the vehicle, and drove off full gallop. Whether the brothers had had scent by some stable-boy or other, that a lady had been at the inn, is not certain; but they had laid watch, the which was easy enough, as there was but one road; but being afraid, they placed themselves in ambush, and suffered them to pass, and followed behind at a small distance expecting to overtake them at the rising of the hill, which was about three miles off, when the horse would be tired. By the time they got within a quarter of a mile from the hill, Gasparo, who was following, leading his master's steed, hearing a trampling of horses, looked back, saw them, and instantly gave the alarm, crying as loud as he could, " Here they are, here they are, we shall have fine sport." Don Nimagri looked out of the window, stopped the carriage, got out, mounted his horse, ordered the postillion to drive as fast as he could out of reach, the which he had no occasion to repeat, for he was gone before Don Nimagri could well turn his horse to face the enemy. The sbirro darting forward, pistol in hand, ordered them to stand. Gasparo, who was more expert at this work than his master, fired his pistol, but missing his aim, only shot the horse : down fell the sbirro. Gasparo dismounted in an instant, put his horse's bridle into his master's hand, ran up to the sbirro, and with his stiletto most charitably put him out of misery, for the poor devil had broken his arm in the fall. Don Nimagri meanwhile fired at the brothers who had advanced upon him. Gasparo seeing the danger of his master in this unequal match, fired his other pistol so successfully, that whether one alone, or both were wounded, was never heard, for both set spurs to their horses, like the valiant knight " who ran away, to live to fight another day."

Don Nimagri finding that the enemy was fled, did not think it necessary to follow them, but turned his

F

attention to the lady.　They rode up to the carriage as
fast as they could, and found the lady in the greatest
terror ; she eagerly enquired whether her brothers were
safe, for cruel as they were, she could not but feel as a
sister, Don Nimagri assured her they had both run
away safe and sound.　There being no time to be lost,
lest they might have run off under the idea of getting
assistance, he ordered the postillion to proceed to the
next post, where they rested some time, the lady being
overcome by the fright, fatigue, and distress of mind.
As soon as she was recovered they set off, and arrived
safe at Benevento, but although it was in the middle of
the night, no entreaty or remonstrance could prevail on
the lady to remain there till morning ; she was so
alarmed at the idea of being surprised, and carried away
by her brothers, whom she had reason to fear were still
pursuing, or perhaps some more powerful dread in the
breast of a virtuous female, now she was discovered,
that with tears she entreated Don Nimagri to proceed
to the convent she had mentioned, to which he reluctantly agreed, apprehending the consternation and
fright such an arrival, and at such an hour, would cre-
ate.　The sisterhood of the convent, as he conjectured,
when they arrived, had just retired again to rest after
their midnight prayer, and were scarcely fallen into a
doze, when they were terrified by the violent ringing of
the great convent bell.　What could be the matter?
was the general cry.　The alarm spread like wildfire;
some fell on their marrow-bones, praying to St. Jenajo ;
some ran with half their garments into the chapel;
some concealed themselves in the vaults, while the

poor abbess lay trembling in her bed, counting her beads. At last the porteress came to the gate, and through the little grating enquired what was the matter. Don Nimagri said that Donna Colomba, the abbess's relation, was pursued, and begged protection. While the good nun went up to deliver the message, the gates were opened, and the chaise drove in. But poor Gasparo was shut out, and thereby exposed to his fate, had there been any one at their heels : but luckily for him, they had been too much terrified to venture a second attack. Shortly after the fugitives were introduced into the chapel, for the abbess seeing the girls running helter-skelter in every direction, did not dare to introduce a man into any room, lest some of them might have sought refuge there. Therefore, into the chapel they went ; two or three of those innocent creatures, who had run into it in their fright, now scampered away as fast as they could, at sight of a man, and at that time of the morning. When the abbess had heard Donna Colomba's account, she thanked Don Nimagri for his very kind and humane attention, expressed great regret at not being able to allow him to stay the night, but offered to send to a neighbouring farm, and obtain accommodation for him and his servant ; entreating him to come in the morning that they might have an opportunity of giving him some testimony of the gratitude they felt for his kind protection to her relation. Don Nimagri, highly pleased at his success in saving the lady, departed. Receiving a message from the abbess in the morning, he attended her, and was presented to the whole sisterhood as the saviour of Donna Colomba's

life and honour, and much gratified with the blessings
and thanks of all these pretty creatures, who vied with
each other in little presents of relics, sweet-meats, &c.
The lady abbess presented him with a very handsome
crucifix set in diamonds.   Donna Colomba could not
find words to express herself, but requested his acceptance of a beautiful diamond ring in remembrance of
her; and loaded him with blessings.   Gasparo, I must
say, was not neglected by the inferior nuns.   Although
not a very prepossessing personage, the account he gave
of his glorious exploits so delighted them, for ladies are
fond of valour, that he did not lack wine, cakes, and the
good things usually met with in convents.   After a few
hours Don Nimagri took leave of the ladies and sisterhood, and arrived safe and sound at Rome.

THE TWO RINGS; A FRENCH TALE.

ALPHONSE, the youngest son of a noble French family, entered the army at an early age: of a warm and
generous disposition, he soon gained the affections, not
only of the officers who commanded him, but likewise
of the men whom he commanded. The country had
for some time enjoyed the blessings of peace, but war
breaking out abroad, the regiment of Alphonse was
ordered on foreign service; the order, which to some
gave uneasiness, on account of families or dear relatives they must leave behind, was to Alphonse a source
of inexpressible pleasure, and his heart panted with
impatience for the moment when they were to embark.
He had an ardent desire to see the world, and that
desire he hoped would now be gratified. He had a
commission to perform for the commander-in-chief at
a town a few miles distant; this of course separated
him from his regiment, which he was to rejoin at ———.
The business was soon performed, and he set forward
on his route, hoping to be at head-quarters before
night. His road lay across the country; the path was
wild and unfrequented: involuntarily he fell into a
train of thought which absorbed his faculties, but he
was suddenly recovered from his reverie by the approach of a lovely girl, apparently between fifteen and
sixteen: her dress was simple, yet such as bespoke her
above the common rank, Never before had Alphonse

found his heart affected by beauty; now it was enslaved in a moment by a stranger. "What an angel is this," thought he, "yet wretched that I am, I only see her to lose her for ever! but no! I will not lose her, she shall be mine, or death shall be the consequence to both." With an ardour and impetuosity that could only be excused in a youth of eighteen, he dismounted from his horse, seized the hand of the young lady, threw himself on his knees before her, and began to pour forth the most rapturous and extravagant expressions of eternal love and constancy. Terrified and alarmed, the lady endeavoured to escape. "Sovereign arbitress of my fate," exclaimed Alphonse, "you must not leave me without some pledge that you will think of me; give me this ring," drawing one off her finger which had the motto of *Souvenez vous de moi*, in small gold letters, encompassed by a wreath of olive. "You may take the ring," said the lady, "only permit me to depart." "First," returned Alphonse, "take mine in return; the motto is *Je viens*, and now you must kneel down, and in the presence of your Creator swear, by every hope you entertain of happiness, in this world, or that which is to come, you will never marry any man but the one who shall present you the ring I have just taken from you; and I, on my part, swear I will never marry any woman but the one who shall have the ring I have just given you; you must likewise swear never to part with it, and never to mention the present adventure—Will you swear?"—"For heaven's sake," said the lady, "let me go; you terrify me beyond expression."—"Angelic creature, be not

terrified, but swear instantly, or you die." He drew
his sword : the affrighted girl threw herself on her
knees, and intreated for mercy. " Swear instantly,"
cried Alphonse, " or death"——" Oh ! I swear I will
never marry any one but you : oh, do not murder me !"
——" I would sooner murder myself: repeat the oath
deliberately.——Now I am satisfied, and I swear by the
honour and valour of a soldier, and by the same hopes
as yourself, never to marry any but the possessor of
the ring you have just received." Alphonse then endeavoured, by the most tender expressions, to calm
the apprehension of the terrified fair, who was near
fainting with fear : when he had tolerably succeeded,
he reluctantly bade her farewell, charged her to be true
to her oath, set spurs to his horse, and was soon out
of sight.

The next day they embarked, and Alphonse recollected, with inexpressible chagrin, that he had not inquired the name of his mistress: he blamed his rash
impetuosity, and even dreaded lest his violence should
have thrown her into a fever that might occasion her
death. With reflections of this nature he passed the
time of the voyage till they arrived at their destination,
when he was obliged to lose, in the horrors of war, the
solicitudes of civil life. His valour endeared him to
all: was any hardy enterprize to be undertaken, Alphonse was always in it,——were the soldiers discouraged
by any disadvantage on their side, Alphonse was sure
to reanimate them, both by words and actions. His
conduct gained him both approbation and promotion.
After a tedious campaign of nearly six years, the regi-

ment was called home, that it might once more enjoy
the comforts of repose.

Alphonse was now in his twenty-fifth year ; the mad
impetuosity of eighteen had but little subsided, and he
passionately longed for the moment when he should
land in his native country, that he might again behold
the maid who had enslaved his heart ; but how he
should discover her was an object of disquiet and solicitude : he did not so much as know her name : for
whom then could he enquire?—she might still reside
at the same place ; it was a forlorn hope, but the only
one he had, and therefore tenderly cherished.

At length they embarked, and after a prosperous
voyage, Alphonse once more beheld his native land ;
he immediately obtained leave of absence for some
months, and after sending a letter to his father, informing him he should soon have the pleasure of
throwing himself at his feet, set forward on the wings
of expectation to find his unknown fair.

The second day, towards evening, he entered the
lane where he had first beheld her ; he dismounted,
and leading his horse, proceeded slowly forward, meditating on the various circumstances which had occurred since that time.

At length he reached the spot where the conference
was held, a conference neither had forgot, or perhaps
could forget ; he reached it, and beheld, not a lovely
young girl, but an old woman gathering sticks.

" My good mother," said Alphonse, " are there any
young ladies live hereabout ?"—" Young ladies," repeated the old woman, looking suspiciously at him,

" what do you want with young ladies ?"—" I left one
here about six years ago : I thought perhaps——"—
" Six years ago! mercy on us! and did you expect she
was to wait here all that time?"—" No, no; but I
thought perhaps you might know her : she wears a
ring——"—" Wears a ring : there's nothing wonderful
in that—many young ladies wears rings: what's her
name ?"—" I do not know her name, but——"—" Not
know her name !" here the old woman fell into a violent laugh, which Alphonse felt too much vexation to
attempt interrupting : at length, recovering, she continued, " to tell you the truth young man, I am afraid
you are after no good, it's a little outré to inquire for a
lady without a name."—" My good woman," said Alphonse, " take this piece of gold, and be so good as to
hear me without interruption : do you think you are
capable of so great an effort ?"—" Ay, your honour,
that I am ; I could hear your honour for two hours
without speaking a word, though your honour knows
speech is very natural to one." Alphonse then gave
her the gold, which she received, with the greatest humility, frequently gazing upon it while he related the
adventure, which was only interrupted by a few exclamations of surprise.

" And now, my good mother, do you think you can
assist my search ? what genteel families reside hereabout ? "—" Very few, the village is about a quarter of
a mile down that narrow path ; there are some genteel
families there, but very few."—" Have any of them
daughters of the age this lady must be, about twenty
one ? "—" No, your honour, none of the young ladies

can be above seventeen."——"You have lived here some years; can you not recollect any family having daughters that might answer my description?"

The old woman considering for some time, then exclaimed, "Holy virgin! I think I can unravel the mystery: there was an English lady kept a boarding-school after the English fashion here, and a pretty piece of work she made of it; the ladies, instead of being kept in as they are in our holy convents, used to be rambling about the fields of a morning and evening, till at last two or three of them ran away with young officers, and one lady, the daughter of some great duke, was carried off by force, and then the lady herself was obliged to fly to England to escape the Bastile."

"Did she take her pupils with her?"——"No, she was glad to get away as she could: she pretended to go to bed as usual in the evening; before one o'clock in the morning a *lettre de cachet* came for her, but my lady was gone, and nobody could tell how, unless the devil had flown away with her, for her door was locked inside and the key left in it."

"That was extraordinary: perhaps she was concealed about the house."——"Not she, your honour: she was on her way to England, and after she had got there she had the impudence to write to the gentlefolks here, that she was safe in her own country beyond the reach of French tyranny."——"What was her name?"——"Her name was Norton."——"She lived in the village you say?" "Yes, your honour, the first on the left as you enter it." Alphonse then thanked the old woman for her information, and took the road for the village: he was not long before he reached it, when he immediately proceeded to the house which had formerly been occupied by Mrs. Norton.

The elegant and prepossessing appearance of Alphonse gained him a ready admittance : he was ushered into the parlour, where he was accosted by an old gentleman, who requested to know his business. " Sir," said Alphonse, " I feel myself in a very awkward situation, and I fear when I inform you of the cause, my conduct will appear very blameable, but I must intreat that you will hear me patiently, and if it is in your power to assist, that you will have the goodness to do it."— " Your frankness pleases me," said the gentleman, " and you may depend on any assistance I can give, consistent with the honour of a gentleman to grant."— " What would not be proper for a gentleman to grant, would not be proper for a gentleman to ask ; but not to trespass on your patience, I will briefly tell you the cause of my giving you this present trouble." Alphonse then related his adventure with the young lady, and also his recontre with the old woman. " And now, sir," continued he, " can you give me any information whereby I may be likely to discover my unknown fair ?" —" If it were in my power," returned Mr. d'Albert, " I should be happy to do it, but unfortunately I have not the least clue to guide your search."—" Can you not inform me in what part of England Mrs. Norton resides ? She sent a letter to some family here."—" She did, it is true, but she gave not the least hint of her residence."—" I beg your pardon, sir, for the trouble I give, but pray were her scholars French or English ! "

——" They were both, sir: the English ladies were sent for by their friends after Mrs. Norton had arrived in England.

Alphonse thus finding all his hopes of intelligence frustrated, could not forbear execrating the unfortunate schoolmistress, whose imprudence was the cause of his present vexation. "Do not," said Mr. d'Albert, "thus yield yourself a slave to passion, and curse a woman who is more to be pitied than blamed : the degree of liberty the ladies enjoyed was not more than in England they might have done with safety ; in an unfrequented place like this, there appeared no danger in permitting an occasional ramble for a mile or two, and it is not always that the sacred walls of a convent can secure those within them from the stratagems of man." Alphonse made some apologies for his warmth of disposition, and after thanking Mr. d'Albert for his civility, was about taking his leave ; this the gentleman would not permit ; it was late, and Alphonse was pressed to stay the night. The oddness of the adventure he had just heard interested Mr. d'Albert, and he wished to be better acquainted with the hero of it.

The evening passed agreeably, the host and the guest equally pleased with each other ; the female part of the family joined them at supper ; the conversation soon became animated, and when Alphonse retired to the apartment assigned him, he found his spirits much better than when he first entered the house ; but this did not continue long ; he was no sooner alone than the image of his lost mistress presented itself to his view, with all the graces which had at first won his heart; then the idea that he might never find her, distracted his brain, and destroyed his rest, so that the morning dawned before the unhappy Alphonse forgot his sorrows in the oblivion of sleep. The slumbers of a lover are generally short and broken: such was the case with our hero, who arose before eight o'clock, pleasing himself with the idea that he might now be in the very apartment formerly occupied by *Perdita*, for so he had named his mistress: under this impression he sought every crevice of the room, hoping he might discover some writing which might tend to elucidate the mystery; but his search was vain; no tender lines appeared on the walls, no concealed door was discovered, and he attended the summons to breakfast with a degree of chagrin he could scarcely conceal.

Mr. d'Albert easily discovered by his countenance the situation of his mind, and while he could not forbear smiling at the romanticity of his passion, he encouraged him to hope. " Madame d'Albert," said he, " was placed in a convent by her guardian with a view to prevent my obtaining her hand; the name of the convent was concealed from me; I did not so much as know whether she were in France, Italy, Spain, or Portugal: for three years, habited as a pilgrim, I wandered in search of her; I permitted my beard to grow to a patriarchal length, and so completely disguised myself that I was in no danger of being detected. I insinuated myself into every convent, and learned not a few of the intrigues carried on in those holy places. At length, when I was on the point of yielding to despair, I was informed by the porteress of a convent in

Spain, that in a few days a novice was going to take
the veil; I inquired the name of the lady, and heard
with an indescribable mixture of joy and grief, that it
was Maria de——.   The porteress was a good-natured
woman, and after much persuasion and some presents,
I prevailed on her to carry a letter to my beloved : this
she did, and also, on my promising her a bottle of
eau de vie, she engaged to contrive an interview that
same night.   I took care to provide a chaise, and a
couple of stout fellows to defend us in case of a pursuit, for I had a strong presentiment that I should effect
the escape of my charmer.   At midnight I repaired to
the porteress, taking with me the liquor, in which I had
infused a tincture that I knew would lull her vigilance
to rest.   The good lady brought me my fair one, and
then drank off a bumper, wishing us happiness, and
in a few minutes was in a profound sleep.   I hastily
threw her veil over my Maria, and we left the convent,
scarcely breathing for fear.   We took the road to Portugal, arrived there without any accident, and were
soon united in the holy bands of matrimony."

" Ah, sir," said Alphonse, " you were a happy
man; I fear I shall not be so fortunate."   Mr. d'Albert
rallied him on his fears, exhorted him not to suffer his
spirits to sink, and, after mutual professions of friendship, our hero left the hospitable mansion of Mr.
d'Albert.   Little pleased with the success of his en-
quiry, Alphonse began his journey to Paris, where he
arrived without any adventure, and was received with
the greatest affection by his family: for some days he
permitted himself to be tolerably happy, but *Perdita*

was not an object to be long forgotten, and he again began to devise means to discover her: with this view he frequented every place of amusement, both public and private. He was soon considered as a man of spirit, and became a great favourite with the ladies. " The chevalier," would they say, " is a very gallant man: he dances with one, kisses one's hand, bows and sighs, but never says any thing particular." This last clause was somewhat of an inuendo to the fair ones: they little thought that while he was paying them so much civility, he was in search of a lost mistress; and when he so politely kissed their hands, it was only that he might have an opportunity of discovering if they wore the ring on which his happiness depended. Thus vainly employed, one month passed away after another without any appearance of discovering *Perdita*: he confided the secret to a few young men, who undertook to assist in the search; they pursued the same methods as himself, and kissing hands soon became a necessary piece of etiquette.

Sometimes he thought of inserting an advertisement in the public papers, she might understand, though to every one else it should be inexplicable; but from this he was deterred by the recollection of the violence which had extorted the oath. " She can have no sentiment for me but fear," thought the unhappy Alphonse: " fear compelled her to take the oath, and fear would now induce her to conceal herself from me if she knew I were in search of her." This expedient was therefore laid aside, and he determined if, at the expiration of three months, he had not found her, to

pursue the search in England, for it was probable she
might be an English lady.   Having made this determination, he felt his mind easier, and prepared to pay
a visit to an uncle who resided about seventy miles
distant from Paris.

It was a beautiful morning in autumn, when Alphonse, attended by his servant, began his route to his
uncle's ; the charming scenery delighted him, and it
was not till near noon that he began to sigh for Perdita.
The sun was now insufferably hot: an inn appeared
in view, and thither Alphonse bent his way, that
he might rest till the heat was over.   The inn-
keeper's daughter, a very handsome girl, brought
in some refreshments : as she was placing them, Alphonse took her hand, and kissed it with the most
profound respect;   the girl blushed, and continued
arranging the table, while Alphonse took up a paper
and began reading, apparently forgetting there was a
girl in the room.   " The gentlemen," thought Alice,
" must be a little deranged."   The circumstance was
related at the table d'hote with much exaggeration,
and furnished the guests with a subject of mirth and
conversation.

The heat of the day being over, Alphonse again set
forward on his journey ; he had not proceeded far, when
he beheld a carriage approach at full speed, the horses
appeared frightened, the postillion had no power over
them, and Alphonse hastened forward to endeavour to
stop their career; at the sight of Alphonse they began
to plunge and rear ; the postillion was thrown to some
distance, the carriage was overturned, the axletree

broken, one horse was killed on the spot, and the other lay panting unable to rise. Alphonse and his servant hastened to render what assistance they could to the unfortunate travellers; an elderly gentleman, and a lady who called him father, were taken from the carriage, very little hurt, but a younger lady, who had borne the weight of these two, was lifted out apparently lifeless. Alphonse threw aside her veil to admit air, and beheld a face at once beautiful and interesting, though overspread with the pallid hue of death. Ever intent on the object nearest his heart, he hastily examined her hands: no ring appeared, and for the first time Alphonse regretted his oath. The usual methods of recovery were tried without success; no signs of life appeared, and Alphonse, with an aching heart, offered to conduct the strangers to the inn he had just left. He then, taking the lady in his arms, (whose weight he scarcely felt), proceeded before them, while the servants of the different parties, leading horses, carrying baggage, &c. brought up the rear of this mournful procession. They soon arrived at the inn; a surgeon was immediately sent for, who, after feeling the pulse of the lady for some minutes, declared that life was not extinct; he judged it necessary to take a little blood, which operation had a happy effect, a deep sigh announcing the return of animation. Alphonse now retired, leaving the lady to the care of her relations: he walked down the inn-yard: the wreck of the carriage was just arrived with the postillion, who was very much bruised: the gentleman's valet was relating the cause of their journey. "We were taking Made-

G

moiselle Louise to a convent, the convent of Mercy too
they called it; but, for my part, I think it a most unmerciful piece of business.   My poor dear young lady
begged and prayed on her knees not to be shut up in a
convent, but my master would not hear her : she must
either marry a man old enough to be her father, or she
must go and be a nun; even Madame Neufville, her
own sister, had no pity for her, but told her she
ought to be obedient to her father.   I thought when
we set out no good would come of it : Mademoiselle
Louise trembled so, she was obliged to be lifted into
the carriage, and when she lost sight of the house she
fainted away: they'll repent of their cruelty when it is
too late, they will."

   " Is it possible," said Alphonse, " they can wish
such a lovely creature as that to be shut up for life?
What can be their motive ?"—" Why, sir, my young
lady has refused several very good offers of marriage,
which affronted my master so much, that he swore if
she did not accept the next, whoever it might be, he
would shut her up for life."—" Poor girl," said Alphonse, " perhaps her heart is secretly engaged."—
" I believe it may, sir, for she is often very melancholy, and sighs as if her heart would break, and
sometimes I've seen her in tears when she thought
nobody saw her.   She's a sweet girl, and I wish some
handsome gentleman of spirit would run away with
her, and save her from a convent."   Alphonse smiled
at the conclusion of the speech and walked away, meditating how he could befriend the unfortunate fair : he
determined at all events to remain at the inn till she

was recovered, that he might, if an opportunity offered, have it in his power to serve her. The next day she was considerably better, and on the third he was admitted into her presence. She thanked him for the care he had taken of her with much elegance, and a degree of confusion that rendered her more charming. Madame Neufville requesting Alphonse to favour them with his company for the evening, he took his seat, and had an opportunity of examining the beautiful features of Louise; the more he gazed, the more he regretted his rash oath, and sighed when he reflected that probably the lady whom he had compelled to swear, might be in the same situation as Louise, forced to enter a convent, or to forswear herself.

" This," thought he, " is the wretched consequence of rash oaths." The evening passed pleasantly in the company of Louise; the convent was not once mentioned, and Alphonse hoped the accident might have induced Mr. Augarde to have laid aside the project, but in this he was mistaken: the next day he was invited to dine with them, and was informed that on the following morning they should recommence their journey to the convent of Mercy. Alphonse gave a deep sigh at the intelligence, which was echoed back by Louise. " Ah, sigh, my dear sister," said Madame Neufville, " the more you sigh when you are a nun the better: you will be canonized at your death, and we shall have Saint Louise."—" She will most likely be beatified before you are out of purgatory," said Alphonse. Madame Neufville coloured; and Louise intreated by her looks that Alphonse would not offend

G 2

her sister : he smiled acquiescence, and was pressing
her hand to his lips, when the long sought for ring
met his eye ; he sunk at her knees, exclaiming in rapture too great for utterance, " *Je suis venu, Souvenez
vous de moi ?*"; " Oh! I could never forget," sighed
the beautiful maid, as she sunk lifeless in his arms.
" What's all this about," exclaimed Mr. Augarde.
Alphonse was insensible to every object but Louise,
whom he feared he had only found to lose for ever. " I
suppose," said Madame Neufville, " you   are   old
friends ! you seem tolerably well acquainted." Louise
was now recovering; Mr. Augarde gazed upon her and
Alphonse, with an air of anxiety.   " Young man," said
he, " I must have an explanation of your conduct; you
appear acquainted with Louise ; relate to me all the
particulars of your intimacy, and if I find you a man
of honour, and you are attached to each other, I give
my free consent to your union; I only wish to see my
child happy."

A vermillion blush overspread the cheeks of Louise,
while Alphonse, with the ingenuousness natural to his
character, related their first rencontre, and his subsequent search, and resolution of visiting England, in
quest of his unknown fair, concluding with relating
the cause of his being on the road, which had happily
conducted him to Mr. Augarde's assistance, and finally
the incident of the ring, which had in one moment
relieved him from a state of uncertainty that was nearly
insupportable, and left him nothing to wish but the
free acceptance of Louise, and the consent of Mr. Augarde to their marriage.   " You have my consent,"

said Mr. Augarde, " but what says my girl? speak my Louise: ' *In sweet disorder lost she blush'd consent,*' while Madame Neufville, with much good humour, congratulated them on the happy termination of the mutual anxiety which had so long embittered the existence of both.

Instead of proceeding to the convent of Mercy, they, the next day, took the road to Paris, where they arrived towards evening. Alphonse conducted them to the hotel of his father, the Marquis de ———, where they were received with the courtesy due to their appearance and introduction. Alphonse was again the hero of his own tale, which occasioned much pleasantry. The marquis consented to the proposed union, and the relations and friends of both parties, (among whom Mr. d'Albert was not forgotten), were invited to be present at the ceremony. The ladies could not sufficiently admire the faithfulness of Alphonse, who, though he could have broken his rash oath without detection, had ever held it sacred, and preserved his heart for her who, they all confessed, was worthy of the gift. If the fidelity of Alphonse was admired by the ladies, not less so was that of Louise by the gentlemen; she had had difficulties to encounter to which Alphonse had been a stranger; persecuted by offended relations, and threatened with the gloom of a cloister, she had still preserved the oath without violation in any of its parts, and they all rejoiced at the éclaircissement which had taken place.

The happy morn which beheld the union of this faithful pair, was ushered in with the demonstrations of joy usual on such occasions. The priest who performed the ceremony was a venerable old man, and while he gave his benediction to the happy couple, he with great solemnity warned the surrounding friends from making rash vows. " Providence," he observed, " had in the present instance permitted that these two should come together, but had it been otherwise, Louise must have spent her life in a cloister, while Alphonse must have dragged on a wretched existence, conscious that it was a state in which he had precipitated himself by presumption and folly."

Deeply affected, the company retired from the chapel, attended by a numerous train of peasantry, who were assembled to rejoice in the general joy; fifty young maidens received marriage portions, and all united in blessing the nuptials of Alphonse and Louise.

THE HUNCH-BACK COBBLER OF VENICE.

AFTER the splendid ceremony of wedding the Adriatic sea, which the chief magistrate of Venice performs by going out in his state-barge and throwing a ring into the waves, a splendid banquet in his palace, and general revelry throughout the city, usually occupy the day. On one of these annual occasions, the doge, having celebrated the allegorical ceremony expressive of his maritime authority, retired to a small supper-table with a few select friends, to enjoy an entire release from official cares. And that it might be fully felt by his guests, he deputed his favourite, Count Annibal Fiesco, to perform the honours of the table, and sat himself among the entertained. The favourite, a nobleman of rich comic humour and grotesque person, compared himself to Sancho Panza in his court of Barataria; and the guests seizing the license of the moment, rallied him gaily on his likeness to that merry squire's exterior.

"Say at once," rejoined the count, "that you think me a tolerable *Panache.*"

The doge asked an explanation of this sally, and was answered with great gravity:——

"Monsignor, the personage I mention is at this time of high importance at the court of France. She is hump-backed, wry-footed, squints prodigiously, takes snuff, scolds everybody, and sits at all tables. One gives her a sweetmeat, another a box on the ear——she mistakes the offender, tells all the truth she knows, and never fails to make mischief. Therefore she delights all the ladies of the court, and whatever ought not be told, is said to be told by Madame Panache. One of these fair ladies was well received by the royal family of Sweden, but unluckily compared the queen to Madame Panache; and the consequence may be guessed, as the queen was an ugly woman."

" Had she been an ugly man," said the chamberlain, slily glancing at the favourite's deformed person, " the revenge would have been different. Instead of ruining the lady's husband, which probably gave her no great concern, I would have sentenced her to wear the hump, and bear the name of Madame Panache. But perhaps she had not wit enough to play a fool's part well."

" Every wise man has not quite wit enough for that," interposed the doge, seeing some symptoms of Italian anger in his friends' faces; and casting a glance at the count, he put on his scarlet cloak, and resumed his place at the head of the table, with an air of mild authority, which seemed to request forbearance. The favourite obeyed it with ready grace.

" Your highness," said he, " shall see how easily a fool's part may be played. No man in this city is said to resemble me, except the cobbler Antonio; and I will wager my best white horse, that in three days I will wear his clothes, handle his tools, and make his grimaces so well, that he shall not be certain whether he is himself, or I am he. Nay, if your highness chooses to have this carnival of folly complete, I will bring him to confess he is a dead man, and that I am his ghost."

The doge staked a hundred ducats on the experiment, and the chamberlain joined in wishing the count success in the farce of " Il Due Gobbi."

An obscure shed, or what in England would be called a cobbler's stall, was the abode in Venice of a cele-brated person called Antonio Raffaelle——not the painter whose talents have excited so many imitators, but a little square-headed, hump-backed shoemaker, whose neighbours gave him this eminent sirname in derision of his ridiculous ugliness and excessive vanity. Almost all the noted artists in Venice had taken this Æsop's likeness, as an exercise for their skill in caricature, but with infinite delight to Antonio, who imagined himself a second Antonius.   One night, after earning a few pieces of coin upon the quay, he returned to his cassino, and was surprised to see a square-headed, hump-backed dwarf, seated by his wife's side, com-posedly eating macaroni, and drinking lemonade.

" In the name of St. Mark," said the high-spirited Italian cobbler, " how comes such an ill-favoured cicis-beo here in my absence ? and how dares he stay when I come home ?"

" Signor Gobbo," replied the dwarf, bowing with great civility and nonchalance, " considering that you have thought fit to counterfeit my hump and my crooked leg, I make no answer to your comment on my ill-looks ; but I take leave to eat my own macaroni, and sit at my own shop-board, without any offence to any gentleman."

Antonio Raffaelle answered this harangue with a very scientific blow, which the new cobbler returned him with such speed, and such sufficient aid from the lady, that his opponent was forced to abandon his household hearth, and fight outside. All the lazaroni of the neighbourhood assembled to see the manual debate ; and as poor Raffaelle was completely vanquished, very wisely, and with the usual logic of a mob, concluded him in the wrong, and joined the imposter in driving him out of the street. Antonio was a practical philosopher, and instead of waiting for farther compliments from the victors, went to the nearest officer of police, and made his complaint.

" This is all very ingenious," said the magistrate, laughing; but my good little Annibal, everybody knows the old cobbler you pretend to be, and his ugliness is a hundred times more comical than your's. I have known the steeple on his shoulder ever since I was a boy, and wrote my lessons twenty years ago, under the inspiration of his genius for lying. Go and add three pounds to that mound on your back, and make a better semicircle of your leg, before you come to me again."

There was no enduring this taunt. Raffaelle ran in a fury of aggrieved honour to Signor Torregiano, an artist, who had just finished a sketch of him, and implored his aid to identify an injured man.

" Ha! ha!" answered the Signor, uncovering his easel, " that will be no difficult matter. His back serves me as the model of Vespasian's arch ; and I shall send for him to-morrow to finish his profile—I want it for the Princess of Parma's museum—and here it is, except the nose, which I have not ochre enough to finish. My wife's parrot mistook it for a cockatoo's beak, and pecked at it."

If Raffaelle was astonished at the insolent raillery of the painter, he was still more confounded when, in reply to his clamorous complaints, the Signor drily ordered his lacqueys to turn the impostor out of doors.

"These rogues think," said the artist, taking a long whip, and bestowing it liberally on his visitor, "that any dwarf may mimic our Raffaelle; but I would have them to know, an ugly knave must be a clever one."

Poor Antonio hardly knew how to believe his own ears, which had been so often feasted with praises of his fine bust, and antique proportion. But one person might certainly be found to bear witness of his identity; and he ran like a tortoise in an ague to the confessional of Father Paulo, a rosy Dominican, whose sandals he had often repaired.

"For the love of justice and St. Dominick," said our persecuted cobbler, "assist a wronged man to confront his enemies. A caitiff, who calls himself Antonio Raffaelle, has entered my house, seized my stock in trade, eaten up my supper, and seduced my wife. And the neighbours say——"

"Ah, very true!" answered the priest, resting his hands gravely on his sides; "what the neighbours tell you is nothing more than the precise truth. I owed him two maravedis for mending my shoes last night; but he had such an enormous bale of sins to confess, that I shall deduct the two maravedis as a penance."

"What, holy father! will you not even pay me for my day's work?"

"Your's, lazarone!—I employ, for my cobbler, a

dull roguish drone, who has more ugliness than Æsop,
and more tricks than all Æsop's birds and beasts; but
his face is so strangely like St. Januarius's phial, that I
verily believe it grows red by miracle, and therefore I
patronise it."

Not even Raffaelle's devout respect for the Catholic
church, could repress his rage at this accumulation of
outrage. He seized on the Dominican's ample sleeve,
which being filled with Naples' biscuits and Parmesan
cheese, caused an unexpected shower of good things
among the ragged group, whose curiosity brought them
to this scene. While the lazaroni scrambled, and the
cobbler talked, two or three soldiers of the doge's guard
laid their hands on him, and carried him to the nearest
prison, accused by divers witnesses of profaning the
ecclesiastic's person by assault; it was in vain to detail
his wrongs, and plead the law of retaliation. The ser-
geant of the police preferred arguments of another kind,
and after making as many indentures on his back as
would have served for the plan of a tessellated pavement, the ministers of justice sent him forth to seek his
home and property again. Of the latter part, as far as
concerned his wife, he had some fears of finding more
than was necessary, and could have dispensed very well
with any restoration of his living stock. But when he
entered the shop, woeful sight!—He beheld new furniture, a new name, a lady gaily dressed, and the pretended
cobbler sitting with a large assortment of shoes before
him. The outrageous reproaches of Antonio were more
like the chattering of a sick ape than the articulations
of human speech. He danced, grinned, shrieked, and

threw his professional tools in all directions, but especially at the head of his faithless wife, who affected the utmost dismay and astonishment. Officers of justice were sent for again, the neighbours gathered together, the street resounded with shouts, and the doge, whose carriage was passing through it, stopped to inquire the cause. He was a man of mirth and good nature; the ridiculous distress of the two cobblers caught his fancy, and he ordered the matter to be brought to speedy trial.

Antonio Raffaelle bustled through the crowd, and called on the doge to hear him speak on the spot. The state-attendants of the equipage would have driven him off; but the doge laughing heartily, invited him to proceed.

" Sire, your excellency knows, that merit of all kinds must have enemies, and the highest tree, as our proverb says, has the crows' nests in it. It is well known to your highness, that no portrait or statute in your gallery has been finished without a comparison with my figure, and this graceless usurper thinks he may rob me of my fame and my patrons, because he has a high shoulder and curved leg. I beseech your excellency to command that he may meet me face to face in your council-room three days hence, and your ten counsellors shall see which of us is the true Raffaelle."

The doge burst into a second fit of laughter. His Council of Ten, the most formal and formidable tribunal in Venice, engaged in the trial of two hunch-backed cobblers, struck him as such ludicrous burlesque, that he determined to regale himself with a full surfeit of the comedy. " Well, Antonio !" said the merry chief ma-gistrate, " collect your witnesses, and digest sufficient evidence. If I can find ten idle counsellors keeping carnival, they shall sit as your judges, and I will be umpire between ' Il Due Gobbi.' "

The crowd dispersed, the pretended cobbler shut himself into his shop in triumph, and the people of the street, with the usual indolence of Italians, forgot the quarrel between the two hunch-back Sosias before night. Antonio was not so passive. He purchased a large wide cloak of an Armenian Jew, composed a beard of very respectable length, and covered one eye with a patch of green leather. High-heeled shoes and a large shawl folded into a turban, altered his stature considerably, and a gaberdine disguised his distorted shape. Thus attired, and furnished with an assortment of suitable wares, he presented himself at the gate of Count Annibal Fiesco, the Rochester of the Venetian court, and inquired if he was at home. Our Antonio had received a hint from the doge's chamberlain, of the wager laid by the count, and determined to retaliate the sport on him and his confederates.

The servants had no leisure to answer such appli-cants. They were engaged in discussing the merits of an extraordinary mountebank, or itinerary merry-an-drew, and disputing which of their own number could perform the cleverest feats.

" For my part," said the major-domo, " I have read of stealing the eggs from a bird's nest while she sat on them, and as yonder is a magpie sitting in that tree, I will shew how easily that trick may be played by boring a hole under the nest."

" Ay," rejoined the page, " but who will play the second part of the same trick, and put the eggs back again, without disturbing her ?"

" Gentlemen," interposed the false Armenian, " that is nothing to a feat I have seen among the Saxon gipsies. Let Monsignor, who has, as I see, a suit of his lord's clothes under his arm, tuck them under mine, and carry my box of small wares to the top of that fine tree. I will engage before you all, and without his perceiving it, to draw off his apparel, and put his master's on his back."

The whole conclave of domestics were enchanted; and the page made haste to fold up his lord's scarlet cloak, embroidered doublet, and white silk hose, into a bundle of convenient size; and that the metamorphosis might completely exhibit the artist's skill, another ran to seek Count Annibal's plumed velvet hat and splendid shoes, which were placed as our Gobbo desired, one on his head, the other in the bundle under his arm. The page with the shew-box of trinkets began to mount slowly first, and the mock conjurer, having slung his bundle very carefully, climbed after him, and contrived with great adroitness to perform one half of his task, while the court-yard rang with shouts of laughter. But while the poor page was most inconveniently perched on the top of the tree, his hands encumbered with the shew-box, and his face full of rueful grimaces at his *dishabille*, Antonio suddenly leaped from one of the branches over the wall, and ran off with his bundle, leaving the servants uncertain whether to pursue him, or to laugh at their comrade's ridiculous position. Antonio had no leisure to enjoy that part of the jest. He retreated with his prize to a secret spot, put on the cloak, rich vestment, and other contents of the bundle, and placing his gemmed and feathered hat with a gallant air on his head, he presented himself at the doge's palace, and entered his council-chamber.

" What, Annibal!—so soon tired of the jest ?" said the merry doge, laughing as he saw him enter,—" But you have not yet fulfilled all the conditions of your wager : you promised not only to dislodge the cobbler from his stall, cheat his neighbours, and usurp his business, but also to convince him he was dead."

" That I shall soon do, for your highness's amusement," replied the counterfeit nobleman, " provided we have the pomp of a formal council, and bring him before us with due judicial ceremony.   The rogue has taken possession of his stall again, and it will not be amiss to send for him with a formidable posse of your officers, and cite his wife also.   We shall need the evidence of two or three other persons, but they must be summoned at a proper time."

The doge renewed his laughter, and bade his favourite follow into his private cabinet.

" This will be a more imposing room of inquisition," said he, taking his chair of state—" You, my chamberlain, and myself, will form a council of three, more terrible in Venice than the ten fools of my larger council."

" That is true," replied the mock count, drily, " and three, including your highness, are quite sufficient: but that my task may be properly fulfilled of frightening this cobbler to death, your messengers must hint that he is charged with a secret conspiracy, revealed, as usual, through the lion's mouth."

The thought was instantly approved and executed ; the council of three took their places near their table in official order, and in half an hour the pretended cobbler was brought in, handcuffed, and placed before them, attended by Antonio's wife.

Our original Antonio folded his scarlet cloak, and adjusted his brows with a scowl of scorn very well befitting a Venetian judge ; and his imitator, not so well understanding this unexpected part of the farce, waited in silence for the result.

" You, who call yourself Antonia Raffaelle, cobbler and seller of monkeys on the Rialto," said the doge, in a stern voice, " you who are accused of secret movements against the state, what reason have you for representing yourself as what you are not ?"

" Your highness knows very well who I am," answered the prisoner with an arch glance, which he meant the doge to interpret.—" And you know, moreover, that I am Antonio Raffaelle, the reformer of your servants' soles, and the model of your sculptors' bodies."

" Fellow," interposed the new judge, availing himself of the doge's permission to conclude the comedy as he pleased, " this is too audacious contumely. Every body knows Antonio Raffaelle, commonly called Gobbo the Cobbler, has been dead and buried three

H

days. Let that woman behind you deny it if she dares."

The hunch-back's wife not being prepared to meet this challenge, knew not what to reply. The three inquisitors urged her to confess if this man was her husband, or an impostor; and her prevarications and confusion produced the most ridiculous answers.

" I have thought, Monsignor," said Antonio, addressing the doge with the bow of a man of rank, and a well-imitated air of supercilious negligence towards the prisoners, " I have remembered a necessary means of reaching the truth and confronting these accomplices. Let us send for Signor Torregiano and the Dominican father Paul."

Both were already in waiting, and made their appearance before the council, more perplexed than alarmed. They had been instructed by the doge's merry favourite how to play their parts in tormenting the poor cobbler, but had received no intimations how to behave towards him to-night.   Therefore, when the doge, with an austere air, inquired if the painter had not been sent for to take a sketch of his features after his death, Torregiano very gravely assented, adding that he meant to compose a bust of Æsop from the outline.   The priest was asked if he had not administered extreme unction and heard his last confession; in which the Dominican, thinking the jest required it, made no hesitation in acquiescing.

. " And moreover," said Antonio, in a loud voice, " as this council absolves all priests from the secresy of the confessional, you will acknowledge that he reminded you of the hundred sequins he received from my lord cham-

berlain for slipping a billet into a dancer's shoe, for
which you gave him absolution, and promised to pay
him back the fifty-five you borrowed?"

Paulo, still supposing all this a part of the concerted
jest, assented to the charge, and signed his name to the
notation made by the council's secretary.

" And you, Signor Torregiano," resumed the hunch-
backed judge, " do you not admit in this august presence, that you promised the dying cobbler thirty silver
ducats for the use of his skull, after his decease, to enrich
your art?——And are you not prepared to pay them to
this poor woman, whose grief for her husband has disordered her memory?"

The painter could do nothing but assent and lay
down the money as required ; after which the pretended
count required the presence of the magistrate who presided over the cobbler's district.   This civilian, whose
conduct to our cobbler had been dictated by the doge's
favourite, came without fear to answer whatever might
be proposed ; and the doge, in the grotesque airs of
overacted authority assumed by his friend, saw only
a fresh proof of his inventive drollery and mimic talent.
The count himself, in his cobbler's garb, could no way
conceive how his patron intended this excess of merri-
ment to end ; but when the magistrate was required
to give his wife a certificate of her widowhood, and to
sign himself an affidavit of the cobbler's death, he began
to apprehend some part of the jest would fall heavily
on his own shoulders.   He was not mistaken.   Having
asked again and again if he was not ashamed to appear
in the cobbler's shape after his death and funeral, and

making no reply, the mischievous judge proposed to ascertain whether he was really a corporal mimic, or an apparition of the deceased, by a sound flagellation. Two servants of the doge applied the test with such force, that the count, not knowing any better way to end the trial, exclaimed—" I am dead !—I am dead ;— I confess whatever his highness pleases."

The doge clapped his hands with a cry of applause ; and the favourite, pulling off his ragged disguise, begged the honest dwarf, who personated him, to take back his own apparel and give him his. But Antonio, made bold by his success, first claimed the money which the priest and painter had promised to pay ; and giving his wife her certificate of widowhood, bade her go in peace, and consider him happily released from her. The doge, highly amused and astonished to find the real cobbler had been sitting by his side, confirmed both the divorce and the payments ; and awarded to him the amount of the wager he had laid ; declaring his favourite the loser, but himself a winner of one merry day by the hunch-back cobbler.

The mock trial of the crooked shoemaker by the doge of Venice, only exhibited the ready talent for stratagem, and deliberate spirit of revenge, often found in the lowest order of Italians. The sequel displayed those national characteristics in a higher and more fatal degree.

Count Annibal Fiesco, by whom that mock trial had been originally caused, was secretly suspicious of the high-chamberlain's share in the catastrophe, and severely piqued at the ridicule it had called upon himself.

He baffled the jest in the most graceful way he could, by being foremost in laughter at his personal resemblance to the grotesque cobbler, and by representing him at masked balls as his favourite character. On one of these occasions, as he returned from a midnight entertainment in the attire of Crispin's disciple, a man started from an obscure corner of St. Mark's square, and whispered,

"You have been dangerously late—we have waited for you more than an hour."

Though the speaker wore a lazaroon's loose and squalid apparel, the count knew the voice and features of his enemy, the doge's chamberlain. Believing this the beginning of some intrigue, he was not unwilling to seize what might retort the jest; and imitating the cobbler's voice with his usual perfection of mimicry, he replied,

"Give me my business, and let me finish it before day-light."

"Take this ring, Raffaelle," returned the chamberlain, "and make haste to the villa Salviati—if the man you meet under the gateway says ' *Yes*,' give him the ring, and he will trust you with a letter—if ' *No*,' return here to me, and I shall have other employment for you."

It was safest to make no answer. Annibal took the ring, now well convinced that his adversary held intimate correspondence with the knavish shoemaker; and satisfied by the right of retaliation, which this certainty seemed to give him, he went courageously to the gateway of the villa, and said to the man who stood under its shadow—" Yes or No ?"

" No!" was his answer, without lifting his head; and Fiesco, disappointed by not seeing the face of the intrigue's other agent, returned to St. Mark's place, determined to pursue the adventure, and trusting to his talents as a mimic to prevent his own detection.

Martini, the doge's chamberlain, stood where he had been left, and shewed a joyful gesture when he saw his messenger return. Not a word was exchanged, except the monosyllable *No*, and Martini beckoned the supposed cobbler to follow him. They went through various obscure bye-ways to the back door of a house from whence Martini brought a large package, which he gave to his companion ; and taking another himself, made him a second sign to follow. Count Fiesco began to dislike his enterprise, and to fear it was not connected with ordinary gallantry, or that it was another stratagem to render him ridiculous. But when his conductor stopped at the garden door of a palace occupied by the French ambassador, his ideas changed. He knew how jealously the Venetian republic viewed any intercourse between its subjects and the agents of a foreign power, and he therefore knew that an officer of state in Venice would not hazard a private visit to an ambassador, without some motive more powerful than a jest. His adversary was a young and gallant man; and the probability so strongly favoured his first suspicion of an intrigue, that Fiesco once more determined to understand the matter, and convert it, if he could, into a means of retrieving his own lost credit. The door was opened, not, as he expected, by a muffled duenna, but by the ambassador himself, wrapped in a plain coat,

with a lantern in his hand. He looked at his visitors
as if he expected a third; and shutting them within
his garden-door, asked if all was concluded.

" Your excellency's word is sufficient, said the
chamberlain: " and here is a farther pledge of my
employer's good faith." He took from Fiesco's shoulders the package they bore, and laid his own on it.

" But where is the other deposit?" inquired the
Frenchman—" Can we not finish the affair to-night?
Notwithstanding the convenient indisposition of your
doge, I can defer my audience of leave no longer."

" Not to-night, Monseigneur, unless——but in a
matter of such high importance, we shall be able to
amuse the senate with excuses for delaying your last
audience till this secret treaty is settled."

" And," answered the ambassador, " it will be, I
hope, a preamble and preparation for public treaties
still more expressive of your master's trust. I give
him, on my own behalf, a guarantee of the friendship
which my sovereign wishes to exist between our
nations."

" I am only authorized," said Martini, in an agitated
voice, " to seal this compact—you are a French nobleman, and will not forget its secresy or its sacredness."

" Neither," rejoined the envoy; " nor shall I forget that I received it from a noble Venetian, an officer
of state, and a prime counsellor of the doge."

Martini opened the red box he had brought without
replying: it contained jewels, and some papers which
the envoy eyed with a glance of triumph; and closing
the lid, put his seal upon it. Fiesco saw the secret

glance, and the feelings of a politician rose within him, mingled with those of his private enmity. Martini was concluding a negociation with the crafty minister of a rival nation, and had probably compromised the welfare of Venice, for some purpose connected with his own ambition. Here, indeed, was an unexpected opening to the revenge which Fiesco's soul had claimed as a right, till it thirsted for it as a banquet. The conversation he heard implied some acquiescence on the doge's part, and he felt a sullen pleasure in finding that the patron who had sacrificed him for a jest, was not incapable of sacrificing his country. While he hesitated between that vindictive pleasure, and the more generous impulse which tempted him to throw off his disguise and arrest Martini, the envoy cast on him a significant glance, and the chamberlain directed him to depart, and wait his return in the square of St. Mark.

This was the crisis of Fiesco's fate. He stopped an instant on the threshold, after the garden-gate had been closed upon him, and strove to overhear their farther conversation; but he only heard the envoy repeat the words he had before addressed to Martini, and they renewed the worst passions in the count's inmost heart.

" An officer of the state !——prime counseller of the doge !"——these titles might have belonged to him, if the ingenious mischief of his rival had not supplanted him. He had never been anything more than the favourite jester of the court, and he loathed the doge even for loving what he knew to be only his lowest talent, and for not discovering the many nobler ones which he felt in his possession. Thus stung by private pique and political jealousy, and justified as he believed by both, he returned to St. Mark's square, not to await Martini's return, but to lodge an accusation against him of traitorous intercourse with the minister of France; then throwing his cobbler's coat and other apparel into the canal, he made haste, muffled in an ordinary cloak, to his own mansion: on the door, in large letters, written with red chalk, he saw this alarming sentence—" *Let those who visit foreigners beware !*"

Had he been watched and detected by some spies of the state inquisition, or was the whole a farce concerted by his enemy to annoy him ? Whatever might be the truth, he had acted indiscreetly. He might be proved to have visited the envoy himself; and the doge, whether he was Martini's dupe or his accomplice, was sufficiently powerful to sacrifice him. But Fiesco's spirit was too proud, and his appetite for vengeance too keen, to be checked by vague apprehension: both were roused rather than repelled, by the mysterious danger which threatened him ; and boldly effacing the inscription, he entered his palace, prepared to await the result.

In less than an hour Martini returned from the French minister's rendezvous, and found the crooked cobbler waiting for him in the square of St. Mark. They went together with long strides to the chamberlain's palace, and had no sooner entered his private cabinet by a back-door, than the cobbler spoke. " You are betrayed. Fiesco has made a worse use of his likeness to me now, that when he cheated me of my wife: he has dropped a letter into the lion's mouth, and the officials will be here in an hour. I saw him, and, by the blessing of St. Mark, they will see something on his door too, unless he rubs out my red chalk."

Martini stood petrified, without listening to Raffaelle Gobbo's long explanation of the accident which prevented his own attendance at the appointed time: "there is no leisure for groans, monsignor," he added, with a grin which shewed how well mischief agreed with his nature, though he hated the inventor :—"let us take the chance we have. Give me the deposit you talked of, and I will carry it through fire and water to the Frenchman's: if there be any thing else in the house not safe for the knaves of office to find, a torch will do the business better than a stiletto."

Martini clenched his hands in agony. He put his ear to another door in the cabinet, listened eagerly, and grew pale as ashes—" Not yet!" he muttered—" Not gone yet!—then there is no hope; but I can—" and he cast a glance of desperate meaning at his own sword, which lay on the table. Gobbo's prompt eye caught the intelligence of his; and putting both his hands firmly on Martini's, he exclaimed—

" No, you are right; it is not yet time for you to use it. I have a shorter and a quicker blade, and it shall never flinch from the service of a man who hates my enemy."

Martini answered by a ghastly look of hesitation

and dismay—" There is no use now for torch or stiletto," he said, instinctively recoiling from the deformed
dwarf's grasp—" a gondola !—a gondola !—would save
us all."

Gobbo grinned with the glee of a goblin, and sprang
out of the window at the same instant that the door
was burst open by the officers of the state inquisitors.
They arrested Martini by virtue of their secret warrant : and, seizing his sword, demanded admittance
into the interior cabinet. His countenance had recovered its firmness from the moment of their entrance.
Turning resolutely towards the balcony, he pointed to
it, and said, with an unfaltering voice, " Gentlemen,
if I had meditated escape, the way was open and the
leap easy ; but there can be no need of flight, when
there is no consciousness of crime : I have committed
none, and know of no right you have to violate my
private chambers: there is the door, here is my poig-
nard, and the first man who enters shall know its
temper." He sprang suddenly from their hold as he
spoke, and placed his back against the door, with a
gesture which proved his determination ; but one of
the officials, more daring and crafty than his companions, instantly threw himself out of the window, and
calling for a ladder, prepared to climb into the balcony
of the next room. The crisis was desperate: Martini,
believing that his own flight would be the means of
forcing these men's attention from their other purpose,
made an audacious leap after him, and ran towards the
canal ; all the officials followed, forgetting the mysterious cabinet, in their zeal to prevent his escape, and

his plunges into the labyrinths of his wooded garden again drew them from the banks of the canal: his own escape, he knew, was utterly impossible ; but he prolonged the struggle in the darkness of his groves, till the dashing of an oar informed him that his point was gained.   Slowly, and with difficulty, he suffered himself to be overcome, and was carried, covered with wounds, to the state prison of the republic.   His violent resistance had given force to the charge exhibited against him; and though neither papers, nor any suspicious articles, could be found in his cabinet when rigorously searched, the correspondence he had held with a foreign minister, contrary to the letter of Venetian law, was too clearly manifest.   The physician of the French envoy had been often seen in his company, and the most severe and artful examination could extort no confession from him; neither affirmation nor denial escaped his lips, and the cruel question warranted by national custom was applied without success. An appeal was made to the ambassador, requesting him to permit the physician of his household to appear before the secret council ; but his reply was a positive refusal, grounded on his privileges, and followed by his departure, with all his suite, from the Venetian territory.   The promptness of this removal, and the ceremonious caution of his answer, indicated, or seemed to indicate, the political importance of the fact.

No one knew, though a few of his friends suspected, the cause of Martini's disappearance from court, and none, except Count Fiesco, rejoiced to observe it.   Even his gloomy rejoicing was not unmingled with fears for his own safety, excited by the writing on the wall, and he remained at his villa in cautious inactivity. A summons to attend the doge brought the cowardice of conscious guilt to his heart; and not daring to disobey, lest his hesitation should convict him in a share of Martini's downfal, he entered his patron's presence. The quiet sadness in the aspect of the good old doge relieved him from fear, and even revived the sullen pleasure of vengeance; but that dark and brief feeling sunk into remorse when the doge squeezed his hand, and wept.

" I sent for you, Fiesco, because I know your affection for me is strong enough to vanquish your dislike to a man I cannot forsake. Here is a testimonial in his favour, written and signed with my own hand, which I require you to read for him in the presence of the council. From no one but yourself have I a right to expect such an effort of courage, and from no other man would it have such force. You are his avowed opponent, therefore you can be suspected of no prejudice in his favour;—you have been always high, perhaps highest in my esteem, therefore you have nothing to gain by his release, except the honour of serving justice and befriending an enemy."

Fiesco's spirit melted at this appeal, and he knelt to kiss the hand which offered him the paper.

" Promise nothing till you have read it, count!—Go, and return to me with your determination."

He would have been unable to form a reply, and retired eagerly to read the contents in the next chamber. They were short, and in this frame of words ·——

" The doge of Venice cannot appear as a witness before the supreme council of his government, nor assent to their decision as a judge, without acknowledging himself a party in the cause.

" Perhaps his selection of Martini to fill the high office of his chamberlain and public secretary, has offended some competitor of more eminent birth and enterprising spirit. Such a competitor has probably been the writer of the anonymous accusation, and the discoverer of Martini's supposed conspiracy with a foreigner. Had this discoverer known all the secrets of the court he has been so ready to disgrace, he would have remembered the disappearance of the doge's daughter. Ippolita's innocent levity of heart led her to the verge of a marriage she secretly repented. On the eve before its completion, her father detected her correspondence with his secretary, and their plan of flight together. The gondola was in waiting at the steps of his terrace, when the doge seized his daughter and confessed himself the father of her lover. She plunged in despair into the canal, and was saved by the desperate efforts of her brother. What was their miserable father's resource?—His only daughter's life was preserved, but her reason seemed to have forsaken her! There were no witnesses of this dismal scene ; and he resolved to circulate a rumour of her death, and consign her to the care of her unfortunate brother. The gondola was ready, her ravings were stifled, and Martini conveyed her to the retirement of his villa. No one doubted her accidental death, or no one ventured to contradict the tale she and her confidants had contrived,

to deceive her father. The scarf and veil were found among the sedges of the canal ; and the scheme she had devised to cover her elopement by pretended death, served as a refuge for her misery. The physicians of the French embassy had known skill and integrity, and the doge of Venice submitted to the grievous necessity of trusting to them. The ambassador agreed to charge himself with the sick princess, and to seclude her safely in a noble convent, if her afflicted spirit revived. Had that cruel spy, who debased himself to watch Martini, understood the purport of his conversation, he would have pitied the anguish of a brother, obliged to surrender his sister to a stranger ; his sister, made insane by the criminal reserve of an erring father, and the too vivid sense of her own virtue. Had the messengers of the council entered his cabinet, which he defended at the risk of his life, they would have seen that miserable father weeping over his only daughter, striving to recall her recollection, and entreating her to accompany him to the asylum he had prepared for her. They would have seen him forced at last to hide her in the gondola brought by a poor faithful wretch, and to leave her, while she clung to him in the helplessness of idiotism. Could he publish her misfortune to a cruel and misjudging world?—Can he blame the noble courage of a son and brother, willing to sacrifice both his life and honour to preserve his family's ?—Shall he see it recompensed by a shameful death, or by tortures and imprisonment, without convincing the council how deeply remorse is felt, though too late, by the doge of Venice ?"

Fiesco read no farther.   He returned into the presence of the doge, and threw himself at his feet, crying,

".No," my lord, it is my task to clear Martini, since my accusation has been the cause of this misery.   I have visited the ambassador—I can take upon myself the whole odium of the offence, without exposing the secret of your family.   Let me prove my love for Ippolita's fair fame equal to Martini's.   Ah! my lord! in this, at least, I deserved to be your son also."

The doge rested his grey hairs on Fiesco's shoulder, and clasped his hands over his head.   The strong ague of mental agony shook his whole body, as he answered,

" Ye had the same father—Ippolita has two brothers."

Fiesco was silent and stiff as in death ; and, after a long pause, his distressed parent added,

" But I have not injured *thee*, my son ; go and atone for me and thyself."

" For myself !" said the count, rousing himself, with the fire of sudden frenzy in his eyes; " am I, who have been your other victim, to be your advocate ?   Shall a father, whose blind pride, or untimely caution, educated me in ignorance of my birth, call on me now to atone for the mischief caused by his false shame ?   Was it the deformity of my figure, or the beauty of my brother's, that raised him to your council, and debased me to the station of your court-buffoon ?   Why was I tempted to love and hate without measure, by living as a stranger among my kindred ?   Should I have been seduced by opportunity to disgrace my rival, had I known he was my brother ? or to endanger my prince, had I been permitted to reverence him as a father? But I will not sacrifice my sister's honour, and my brother's blood shall not rest on my head."

Fiesco disappeared, leaving the paper among the burning ashes on the hearth, and his father frozen with dismay and horror. That night the Council of Three passed sentence of death on Martini, for whom no advocate appeared, and ordered his immediate execution. But the black gondola, employed to convey the state's secret victims to the fatal lagoon, was seen hastening towards the Adriatic coast, rowed by two goblin dwarfs, and returned no more. A stone in the cemetery of a Bolognese convent bears the name of Ippolita, and was permitted, also, to cover the remains of an unknown soldier, who fought and died in the army of the doge of Venice.

THE BROTHERS OF DIJON.

THE president of the parliament of Dijon and the bishop of Beauvais disputed, one evening, on the strange and desperate actions frequently committed by men of characters long approved and generally exemplary. " I have thought of this inconsistency," said the president, " till I have almost convinced myself that we have two souls; one which directs or attends only the mechanical and every-day business of our bodies, and a superior one which never acts unless excited by some peculiar things addressed to our feelings or passions. You and I must remember that we have often wrote, read aloud, drawn, ate, talked, and dressed ourselves, without any consciousness or idea; and these operations appear to me directed by, what I fancifully call, the soul of our bodies, while the soul of our minds is otherwise employed. If the notion or name of two souls displeases you, we will call them habit and impulse; but I conceive the last to be the result of our thoughts and feelings, the other of mere mechanical instinct. And I conceive this impulse, or soul of our thoughts, to be as capable of suddenly inciting actions contrary to our general habits, as those habits are often practised without the assent and presence of our thoughts."

The bishop was offended by this metaphysical subtlety. " Do you mean to tell me," said he, " that the natural impulses of men are wicked, whatever may be their general habits, and that such impulses are beyond control ?"

I mean," continued the president, " that the sudden actions of men proceed from the general bent of their thoughts, not of their common conduct; therefore I judge by such actions of a man's real temper, rather than by his every-day duties and behaviour. And knowing that we are too apt to give our secret thoughts full license, provided our actions are well regulated, I am not surprised when sudden temptation produces violent and scandalous acts in those whose ordinary conduct is decent, because premeditated or mere method."

The prelate shook his head. " Perhaps," he replied, " I ascribe too much influence to reason, and you too little to temptation. We may both see and experience occasions when temptation creates thoughts never felt or indulged before, and when opportunity steps before judgment. I humbly trust to right habits as the best preservatives from wrong impulses, and I leave you to determine your belief by facts ; though it is my belief, no less than your's, that no man's habits will be consistently and constantly good, whose thoughts are wandering and unregulated."

Soon after this conversation the bishop left his brother, and returned to his hotel, or temporary residence, in Dijon. On the threshold, under the light of a few straggling lamps, he saw a stranger of mean appearance, who put a small billet into his hand, and waited respectfully while he looked into it. It was badly spelt and written, but purported to be from a dying woman in great need of spiritual help, and especially desirous to communicate with him at the corner house of the rue St. Madelaine. The bishop knew this street to be situated at no great distance, in an honest though poor suburb, and the requested visit could be attended by no danger. Even if it had, the prelate had enough of benevolent courage to hazard something in his professional duty, and he desired the stranger to conduct his coachman. Alighting at the entrance of the narrow lane which led to the rue St. Madelaine, and was too narrow to admit his equipage, the bishop desired his servants to await him there; for though he had too much charitable delicacy to desire parade in his visits of bounty, he also felt that his official station as a public instructor required him to shun all mysterious or questionable acts. Therefore directing his guide to take a flambeau from his lacquey, he followed him to the appointed door, and more particularly noticing the house, observed that its back wall overlooked the garden of a mansion occupied by a family he knew; the family, in short, from which his brother had selected his future wife, Therese Deshoulieres, a woman of noted beauty and high pretension. Perhaps this circumstance diverted his ideas so far as to prevent him from remarking the disappearance of his guide when he had unlocked a door, which, the bishop entering, found himself in a room very dimly lighted, and without furniture, except a bench on which a woman was sitting. She was muffled in a veil which she drew still closer to her face, but he immediately recognized the air and figure of

Therese Deshoulieres. She appeared no less dismayed and confounded, though she found courage to accost him—" Ah, my lord !—do not believe that I meet you intentionally; the man who just now brought you, decoyed me here by this forgery"—and she put into his hand a billet which seemed the counterpart of that he had received. It was in the same hand-writing, and nearly the same words; but the confusion in the bishop's ideas made him return it in silence. " My servant accompanied me," continued the lady, " and is waiting in the house—surely, my lord, you have not devised this scene to afflict me ! The people I expected to see were sick and in distress, and I came because I feared nothing from honest poverty."—" Therese," said the bishop sorrowfully, " if you had not once feared honest poverty, we need not have feared to meet each other now."—The lady wept ; and though he began to doubt whether the whole was not the finesse of some feminine purpose, her tears were not without effect. But he did not misplace his confidence in the influence of right habits against sudden impulse; for his thoughts of Therese Deshoulieres had been so long governed and corrected, that this unexpected test did not disorder them. " I have nothing," he added, " to say to my brother's betrothed wife in fear and in secret ; nor anything to desire from her, except that ring which she accepted once for a different purpose, and ought not to wear with her husband's." And, as he spoke, he approached to draw the ring from her finger on which he saw it glistening. A dimness came over Therese's eyes; and when it vanished, the bishop was gone, but had not taken the ring from the hand she held out to him. She sat down on the only bench in the room, and wept a long time bitterly and trembling. In a few moments more, she remembered that her servant had been ordered to wait till the clock struck seven before he enquired for her. Her repeater sounded that hour, but Mitand did not appear. She dared not open the door to go alone into the street, but the casement was unbarred, and it looked into her father's garden. She climbed out, and by the help of a few shrubs clinging to the wall, descended in safety, and made haste to the house, hoping her absence was undiscovered. But Mitand had already reached it, and alarmed her family by saying that he had expected to find his young mistress returned. Therese answered her father's angry questions by stating the simple truth—that she had been induced to visit the poor gardener's widow by a billet begging her immediate presence for a charitable purpose, and had found the little lodge empty of all furniture; but a young man who called himself her grandson, had requested Therese to wait a few moments while the widow came from her bed in an upper room. Mitand informed his master that he had waited at the door till a man in a gardener's habit bade him return home, as his lady would go by a back way through her father's garden. M. Deshoulieres blamed his old servant's careless simplicity, and asked his daughter if no other person had appeared : Therese faltering, and with a failing heart, replied, that a man had entered and demanded her ring ; but being informed that her servant was stationed within hearing, had departed without further outrage. This prevarication, so near the truth, yet so fatally untrue, was the impulse of the moment. Therese had never before uttered a falsehood on an important occasion, but her thoughts had been long familiar with the petty finesse of female coquetry; and the step from small equivocations to direct untruth only required a spur.

To colour her evasion, Therese had concealed her ring among the garden shrubs; and professing that she had willingly yielded it to the thief as a bribe for his quiet departure, she entreated her father not to make such a trifle the subject of serious investigation. M. Deshoulieres, seeing no reason to doubt her sincerity, and fearing that an appeal to the police might compromise her reputation, agreed to suppress the matter; but he communicated it to his intended son-in-law, the president of the provincial parliament, who looked very gravely at the forged billet, and asked a particular description of the ring. Then, as he gallantly said, to atone for her loss, he sent Therese a splendid casket of jewellery, which, with some gratified vanity, she added to the celebrated set she inherited from her mother; and a few days after, she accompanied him to the church of St. Madelaine, where the bishop, who had visited Dijon for that purpose, performed the nuptial ceremony.

One of the most splendid fêtes ever seen in that province distinguished the bridal evening. The president, high in public esteem and flourishing in fortune, was attended, according to the custom of his country on such occasions, by the principal persons of his own class, and by all his kindred and friends in the neighbour-

hood.   The bishop remained in the circle till a later
hour than usual, and perhaps with a more than usual
effort, because he was aware a few persons in that
circle knew the attachment of his youth to Therese
Deshoulieres.   But even his brother did not know that,
being a younger son, he had been induced, for the
benefit of his family, to enter the church, and renounce
a woman whose pretensions were far above his honest
poverty.   Therefore on this occasion he affected, with
some little pride, an air of perfect serenity ; and though
he had felt his forehead burn and freeze by turns, he
knew his voice had never faltered while he pronounced
a benediction on the marriage.   He was pledging his
brother after supper, when cries of fire were heard in
the house.   The great profusion of gauze ornaments
and slight erections for the ball made the flames rapid
beyond all help.   Even the crowd of assistants prevented any successful aid ; for the number of timid
women covered with combustible finery, and men unfitted by wine for personal exertion, disturbed those
who came to be useful.   " Is Therese safe ?" was everybody's cry, and everybody believed she was, till the
outline of a woman seen among the flames and smoke
at her chamber-window made the spectators redouble
their shrieks.   The bridegroom would have plunged
again into the ruins, if his brother had not held him
desperately in his arms : but the valet Mitand, who had
lived with M. Deshoulieres from his daughter's infancy,
ran up the remains of the staircase and disappeared.
In another instant the roof fell in, and Mitand was seen
leaping from a burnt beam alone. He was wrapped in a

large blanket which had saved his person, but his neck, hands, and head, were hideously scorched. When surrounded, and questioned whether he had seen his mistress, he wrung his hands, and shook his head in despair; they understood, from his dumb anguish, that he had seen her perish, and he remained obstinately sitting and gazing on the ruins till dragged away; the despair of the president was beyond words, and his brother's utmost influence could hardly restrain him from acts of madness. When the unfortunate bride's father deplored the festival which had probably caused its own dismal end, the president declared, with a fearful oath, that he knew and would expose the author. From that moment his lamentations changed into a sullen kind of fierceness, and he seemed to have found a clue which his whole soul was bent on. It was soon unfolded by the arrest of a young man named Arnaud, whose conveyance to prison was followed by his citation before the parliament of Dijon, as an incendiary and a robber. M. Deshoulieres gave private evidence to support these charges; but a day or two preceding that appointed for a public examination, the president went to the intendant of the province, and solemnly resigned his chair in the judicial court: " it is not fitting," said he, " that I should be a judge in my own cause, and I only entreat that I may not be summoned as a witness."

" No," added the president, as he returned with his brother, " it is not fit that I should be called upon to identify that man, lest his real name should be deemed enough to convict him of any guilt. It is sufficient for me to know him: we will not prejudice his judges."

The parliament of Dijon assembled with its usual formality, and the intendant-general of the province was commissioned to act as president on this occasion. The bishop and his brother sat in a curtained gallery, where their persons might not fix or affect the attention of the court: the bereaved father was supported in a chair as prosecutor, and the prisoner stood with his arms coolly folded, and his eyes turned towards his judges.

The first question addressed to him was the customary one for his name. "You call me," said the prisoner, "and I answer to the name."

"Is it your real name?"

"Have I ever been known by any other?"

"Your true appellation is Felix Lamotte," said the procureur-general—"and I crave permission of the court, to remind it that you stood here ten years ago on an occasion not much more honourable."

The ci-devant president handed a paper to the procureur, requesting that nothing irrelevant to the present charge might be revived against the prisoner.

"Messieurs," said the public accuser, addressing himself to the judges, "I humbly venture to assert, that what I shall detail is not irrelevant, as it may exhibit the character of the accused, and give a clue to his present conduct. Felix Lamotte is the nephew of a financier well remembered in Dijon, and his prodigality gave such offence that his uncle threatened to disinherit him, and leave his great wealth to his most intimate friend, the president of this court. But he, after repeated intercessions and excuses for this young man, prevailed on the elder Lamotte to forgive him. When the nephew heard his uncle's will read, he found the president distinguished by only a legacy of ten thousand livres, and himself residuary legatee. You expect messieurs to hear that Felix Lamotte was grateful to his mediating friend, and careful of his unexpected wealth. He appeared to be grateful until he became poor again by his prodigality. Then, finding a flaw in his uncle's will, he came before this tribunal to dispossess his friend of the small legacy he enjoyed, believing that, as heir at law, he might grasp the whole. The president, who had not then reached his present station among our judges, appeared as a defendant at this bar with a will of later date, which he had generously concealed, because the testator therein gave him all, charged only with a weekly stipend to his prodigal nephew. These are the facts which the president desired to conceal, because the ungrateful are never pardoned by their fellow creatures, nor judged without rigour. We shall see presently how the accused showed his repentance."

"Stop, sir!" said Felix Lamotte, haughtily waving his hand to command silence, "I never did repent. The president created my error by concealing the truth. If, instead of permitting me to rely on a will that had been superseded, he had shown me the last effectual deed of gift, I should have known the narrowness of my rights, and the value of whatever bounty he had extended. He wished to try my wisdom by temptation, and I have mended his by showing him that temptation is always dangerous."

" What you admit, is truth," rejoined another advocate——" though more modesty would have been graceful. But the bent of your thoughts must have been to meet the temptation."

The prisoner answered coldly, " It may be so ; and as that accords with the president's metaphysics, let him thank me for the demonstration."

" Where," said the intendant-general, " have you spent the last ten years ?"

" Ask the president," retorted Felix Lamotte——" he knows the verdict he obtained made me a beggar, and a beggar who reasons metaphysically will soon be tempted to become an adventurer. I have been what this honourable court made me, and I love to reason like the president."

Mitand, M. Deshoulieres' old servant, was called into the court, and asked if he had ever seen Lamotte. He was hardly recovered from the injuries he had received in the fire, but he took his oath, and answered in the affirmative distinctly. Being desired to say where, he said, " in a gardener's dress, at a house in the suburb of St Madelaine, on the night of the marriage."

The accuser's advocate now related all the circumstances of Mademoiselle Deshoulieres' visit to a house without inhabitants, where she had been robbed of a valuable diamond. A pawnbroker appeared to testify that he had received from Felix Lamotte the ring identified as Therese's, and several witnesses proved the billet to be his hand-writing.

" You should also remember," added Lamotte, looking sternly at the pawnbroker, " what account I gave you of that ring. I told you I had found it among the shrubs under the wall of an empty hut adjoining Deshoulieres' garden. My necessity forced me to sell it for bread. Had you been honest, and able to resist a tempting bargain, you would have carried it back to the owner.

" Notwithstanding this undaunted tone," said the procureur, " the prisoner's motive and purpose are evident. Vengeance was the incitement—plunder was to have been the end. To unite both, he has fabricated letters, outraged an unprotected lady, and introduced devastation and death into the house of his benefactor, in hopes to seize some part of the rich paraphernalia prepared for his bride. He hated his benefactor, because undeserved favours are wounds ; he injured him because he could not endure to be forgiven and forgotten."

" I have no defence to make," resumed Lamotte, " for the faults of my youth have risen against me. You would not believe me if I should swear I did not rob Therese, that I wrote no billets to decoy her, that I came into the vestibule of her father's house only to be a spectator of her bridal fête. I lodged in the hut of the gardener's widow, and, unhappily, complied when she solicited me to write petitions for the aid of the bishop of Beauvais and M. Deshoulieres' daughter. This woman and her family removed suddenly, and I am the victim."

" Man," said M. Deshoulieres, stretching out his

arms with the rage of agony, " this is most false. The treacherous billet was written and brought by thy own hand, and here is another charging me to watch and witness my daughter's visit."

" Well, returned the prisoner coldly, " and what was my crime ? If I thought the marriage ill-suited, and without love on the lady's part, was I to blame if I gave her an interview with her first lover ! The bishop of Beauvais can tell us whether such interviews are dangerous."

" Let him be silenced !" interposed the intendant-general ; " this scandal is sacrilege both to the living and the dead. If we had any doubt of his guilt, his malignity has subdued it."

The votes of his judges were collected without any farther hearing, and their sentence was almost unanimous. Felix was pronounced guilty, and condemned to perpetual labour in the galleys ; a decree which the president heard without regret, but his brother with secret horror, when he remembered that Therese might not have spoken truth to her father—yet he respected her memory fondly ; and fear to wound it, more than his own honour, had induced him to give no public evidence. But he had satisfied his conscience by revealing all that concerned himself to the intendant-general, who saw too much baseness in Lamotte's character, to consider it any extenuation of his guilt. Lamotte was led to the galleys, a victim to his revengeful spirit : and the president was invited by his sovereign to resume that seat in the parliament of Dijon which he had so nobly vacated.

Fifteen years passed after this tragical event, and its traces had begun to fade. The father of Therese was dead, and his faithful servant lived in the gardener's house on an ample annuity given to him for his zeal in attempting to save her life. The president, weary of considering himself a widower, chose another bride, and prevailed on his brother to emerge from his retirement and bless his marriage. Another fête was prepared almost equal to the last; but, perhaps, a kind of superstitious fear was felt by all who remembered the preceding. The bishop retired to his chamber very early, and the bridal party were seated in whispering solemnity, when the door opened slowly, and a figure, clothed in white, walked into the centre. Its soundless steps, glazed eyes, and deadly paleness, suited a supernatural visitor; and when, approaching the bride, it drew the ring from her finger, her shriek was echoed by half the spectators. At that shriek the ghostly intruder started, dropped the ring, and would have fallen, if the president's arms had not opened to prevent it. He saw his brother's sleep had been so powerfully agitated as to cause his unconscious entry among his guests; and, conducting him back to his chamber, waited till his faculties were collected. "Brother," said the bishop, " it seems as if Providence rebuked my secresy, and my vain attempt to believe that opportunity and temptation cannot prevail over long habits of good, and be dangerous to the firmest." Then, after a painful pause, he told the president of his secret interview with Therese, his resolution to take back the ring, and the failure of his resolution. He explained how long and deeply this scene had dwelt on his imagination, how keenly it had heightened his interest in the trial of Lamotte; and, finally, with how much force it had been revived by the second marriage-day of his brother. "And now," added the bishop, " I may tell you that its hold on my dreaming fancy may have been lately strengthened by. an event which I wished to suppress till after this day, lest it should damp the present by renewing your regret for the past. Only a few hours since, I was summoned. once more to that fatal house in the suburb to see a dying sinner. I found old Mitand on his death-bed.. He told me that he could no longer endure the horrible. recollections which your wedding-day brought. He. reminded me of the attempt to reach Therese's room when full of flames. At that moment no thought but her preservation had entered his mind; but he found her on the brink of the burning staircase with her casket of jewels in her hand. Miserable Therese! she had thought too fondly of the baubles; and he, swayed by a sudden, an undistinguishing and insane impulse, seized the casket, not the hand that held it, and she sunk. In the same instant his better self returned— all his habits of fidelity to his master, of love to his young mistress—but they came too late. He had thrust his dreadful prize under his woollen wrapper—it remained there undiscovered, while shame, horror, and remorse, prevented him from confessing his guilt. He buried it under the threshold of the garden house which his master gave him with a mistaken gratitude, which heaped coals of fire upon his head. There it has remained with the locks untouched fifteen years, and from thence he wishes you to remove it when you can resolve to speak peace to a penitent.''

Mitand died before morning, and the president's first act was to place this awful evidence of human frailty on the records of the parliament. Their decree against Felix Lamotte was not revoked, as its justice remained unquestionable in the chief points of his guilt : but the fatal influence of temptation over Mitand and the bishop of Beauvais, was a warning more tremendous than his punishment.

K

THE PHYSICIAN OF MILAN; OR THE COUNTERPARTS.

> " One of these men is genius to the other."
> *Comedy of Errors.*

MESSER BASILIO, of Milan, who had fixed his residence in Pisa, on his return from Paris, where he had pursued the study of physic, having accumulated by industry and extraordinary skill, a good fortune, married a young woman of Pisa, of very slender fortune and fatherless and motherless; by her he had three sons and a daughter, who in due time was married in Pisa; the eldest son was likewise married, the younger one was at school; the middle one, whose name was Lazarus, although great sums had been spent upon his education, made nothing of it; he was naturally idle and stupid, of a sour and melancholy disposition; a man of few words, and obstinate to such a degree, that if once he had said NO to anything, nothing upon earth could make him alter his mind. His father finding him so extremely troublesome, determined to get rid of him, and sent him to a beautiful estate he had lately bought at a small distance from town. There he lived contented, more proud of the society of clowns and clodpoles, than the acquaintance of civilized people. While Lazarus was thus living quietly in his own way, there happened about ten years after a dreadful mortality in Pisa; people were seized with a violent fever, they then fell into a sleep suddenly, and died in that state. The disease was catching; Basilio, as well as other physicians, exerted their utmost skill, as well for their own interest as the general good; but ill fortune would have it that he caught the infection and died. The contagion was such that not one individual of the family escaped death, except an old woman servant. The raging disease having ceased at last, Lazarus was induced to return to Pisa, where he inherited the extensive estates and riches of his father. Many were the efforts made by the different families to induce him to marry their daughters, notwithstanding they were aware of his boorish disposition; but nothing would avail. He said he was resolved to wait four years before he would marry; so that his obstinate disposition being well known, they ceased their importunities. Lazarus intent upon pleasing himself alone, would not associate with any living soul. There was, however, one poor man, named Gabriel, who lived in a small house opposite to him, with his wife Dame Santa. This poor fellow was an excellent fisherman and bird-catcher, made nets, &c., and what with that, and the assistance of his wife, who spun, he made shift to keep his family, consisting of two children, a boy of five, and a girl of three years old. Now it happened that this Gabriel was a perfect likeness of Lazarus; both were red haired, had the same length of beard, every feature, size, gait, and voice so perfectly alike, that one would have sworn they were twins; and had they both been dressed alike, certainly no one but

.would have mistaken the one for the other; the wife herself would have been deceived but for the clothes, those of Lazarus being fine cloth, and her husband's of coarse wool of a different colour.   Lazarus, observing this extraordinary resemblance, could not help fancying that there must be something in it, and began to familiarise himself with his society, sent his wife presents of eatables, wines, &c., and often invited Gabriel to dinner or supper with him, and conversed with him. Gabriel, though poor and untaught, was shrewd and sagacious, and knew well how to get on the blind side of any one; he so humoured him that at last Lazarus could not rest an instant without his company.   One day, after dinner, they entered into conversation on the subject of fishing, and the different modes of catching fish, and at last came to the fishing by diving with small nets fastened to the neck and arms; and Gabriel told him of the immense numbers of large fish which were caught in that manner, insomuch that Lazarus became very anxious to know how one could fish diving, and begged of him to let him see how he did it.   Upon which Gabriel said he was very willing, and it being a very hot summer's day, they might easily take the sport, if he too were willing.   Having risen from table, Gabriel marched out, fetched his nets, and away they went. They arrived on the borders of the Arno, in a shady place surrounded by elders; there he requested Lazarus to sit and look on.   After stripping, and fastening the nets about him, he dived in the river, and being very expert at the sport, he soon rose again with eight or ten fish of terrible size in his nets.   Lazarus could not think how it was possible to catch so many fish under water; it so astonished him, that he determined to try it himself. The day was broiling hot, and he thought it would cool him. By the assistance of Gabriel he undressed, and the latter conducted him in at a pleasant part of the shore, where the water was scarcely knee-deep. There he left him with nets, giving him charge not to go farther than the stake which he pointed out to him. Lazarus, who had never before been in the water, was delighted at its coolness, and observing how often Gabriel rose up with nets full of fish, bethought himself, one must see under as well as above water, otherwise it would be impossible to catch the fish in the dark; therefore, in order to ascertain the point, without thinking of consequences, he put his head under water, and dashed forward beyond the stake. Down he went like a piece of lead; not aware he should hold his breath, and knowing nothing of swimming, he struggled hard to raise himself above the surface. He was almost stifled with the water he had swallowed, and was carried away by the current, so that he very shortly lost his senses. Gabriel, who was very busy catching a great deal of fish in a very good place, did not care to leave it; therefore poor Lazarus' after rising half dead two or three times, sunk at last never to rise again. Gabriel, after he had got as much fish as he thought would do for him, joyfully turned round to show Lazarus his sport; he looked round and did not see him; he then sought him everywhere, but not finding him, he became quite alarmed, and terrified at the sight of the poor fellow's clothes that were laid on the bank. He dived, and sought the body, and found it at last driven by the current on the beach ; at the sight he almost lost his senses ; he stood motionless, not knowing what to do, for he feared that, in relating the truth, people would think it was all a lie, and that he had drowned him himself in order to get his money. Driven thus almost to despair, a thought struck him, and he determined to put it in instant execution. There was no witness to the fact, for every one was asleep, it being the heat of the day ; he therefore took the fish, and put them safe in a basket, and for that purpose took the dead body on his shoulders, heavy as it was, laid him on some grass, put his own breeches on the dead limbs, untied the nets from his own arms, and tied them tight to the arms of the corpse: this done, he took hold of him, dived into the water, and tied him fast with the nets to the stake under water: he then came on shore, slipped on Lazarus's shirt and all his clothes, and even his fine shoes, and sat himself down on a bank, determining to try his luck first in saving himself from his perilous situation, and next to try whether he might not, from his extreme likeness to Lazarus, make his fortune and live at ease.

Being a bold and sagacious fellow, he immediately undertook the daring and dangerous experiment, and began to cry out with all his might and main, " Oh ! good people, help ! help ! run and help the poor fisherman, who is drowning.'' He roared out so that at last the miller, who lived not far off, came running with I know not how many of his men. Gabriel spoke with a gruff voice, the better to imitate that of Lazarus, and weepingly related that the fisherman, after diving and catching a good deal of fish, had gone again, and that as he had been above an hour under water he was afraid he was drowned; they inquiring what part of the river he had gone to, he showed them the stake and place. The miller, who could swim very well, rushed in towards the stake, and found the corpse, but being unable to extricate it from the stake, rose up again and cried out, " Oh! yes he is dead sure enough, but I cannot get him up by myself:" upon which two others stripped, and got the body out, whose arms and limbs were lacerated by the nets which (as they thought) had entangled him, and caused his death. The news being spread abroad, a priest came, the corpse was put in a coffin and carried to a small church, that it might be owned by the family of Gabriel. The dreadful news had already reached Pisa, and the unfortunate wife, with her weeping children, came to the church; and there beholding her beloved husband, as she thought, she hung over him, wept, sobbed, tore her hair, and became almost frantic, insomuch that the bystanders were moved to tears.

Gabriel, who was a most loving husband and father, could scarce refrain from weeping, and seeing the extreme affliction of his wife, came forward, keeping Lazarus's hat over his eyes, and his handkerchief to his face, as it were to wipe away his tears, and approaching the widow, who took him, as well as others, for Lazarus, he said, in the hearing of all the people, " Good woman, do not give way to such sorrow, nor weep so, for I will not forsake you; as it was to oblige me, and afford me pleasure, that he went a fishing to-day against his inclination, methinks it is partly to me he owed his death, therefore I will ever be a friend to thee and thine; all expenses shall be paid, therefore return home and be comforted, for while I live thou shalt never want; and should I die I will leave thee enough to make thee as comfortable as any of thy equals." Thus he went on, weeping and sobbing, as if regretting the loss of Gabriel, and really agonized by the distress of his widow. He was inwardly praised by all present, who believed him to be Lazarus.

The poor widow, after the funeral was performed, returned to Pisa, much comforted by the promises of him whom she considered as her neighbour Lazarus. Gabriel, who had been long acquainted with the deceased's ways, manners, and mode of living, entered Lazarus's house as if the master of it; without uttering a syllable ascended into a very beautiful room that looked over a fine garden, pulled out of the dead man's coat he had on a bunch of keys, and opened several chests, and finding some smaller keys, he opened several desks, bureaus, money chests, and found, independent of trunks filled with cloth, linen, and jewels, which the old father, the physician, and brothers of the deceased had left, nearly to the value of two thousand gold florins and four hundred of silver. He was in raptures all the night, and began to think of the best means to conceal himself from the servants, and appear as the real Lazarus.

About the hour of supper he came out of his room, weeping; the servants, who had heard the dreadful situation of the widow Santa, and that it was reported that their master had partly been the cause of the accident, were not much surprised at seeing him thus afflicted, thinking it was on account of Gabriel. He called the servant, and desired him to take a couple of loaves, two bottles of wine, and half his supper to the widow Santa, the which the poor widow scarcely touched. When the servant returned, Gabriel ordered supper, but ate sparingly, the better to deceive the servants, as Lazarus was a very little eater; then left the room without saying a word, and shut himself up in his own room as the deceased used to do. The servants thought there was some alteration in his countenance and voice, but attributed it to the sorrowful event that had occurred. The widow, after having tasted of the supper, and considering the care that had been taken of her, and the promises made by Lazarus, began to take comfort, parted with her relations, who had come to condole with her, and retired to bed. Gabriel, full of thought, could not sleep a wink, and got up in the morning at Lazarus's usual hour, and in all things imitated him. But being informed by the servants that Santa was always in grief, weeping and discomforted, and being a fond husband, and loving her tenderly, he was miserable upon hearing this, and determined to comfort her. Thus resolved, one day after dinner he went to her, and found a cousin of hers with her. Having given her to understand he had some private business with her, the cousin knowing how much she was indebted to him, and her expectations, left the room, and departed, saying, he begged she would be advised by her worthy neighbour.

As soon as he was gone he shut the door, went into his room, and motioned her to follow; she, struck with the singularity of the case, and fearing for her honour, did not know what to do, whether she should or she should not follow; yet thinking of his kindness, and the hopes she had from his liberality, and taking her eldest son by the band, she went into the room, where she found him lying on a little bed, on which her husband used to lie when tired; upon which she started and stopped. Gabriel, seeing her come with her son, smiled with pleasurable feelings at the purity of his wife's conduct; one word that he uttered, which he was in the habit of using, staggered the poor Santa, so that she could not utter a syllable. Gabriel, pressing the poor boy to his breast, said, " Thy mother weeps, unaware of thy happy fate, her own, and her husband's." Yet not daring to trust himself before him, though but a child, he took him into the next room, gave him money to play with, and left him there. Returning to his wife, who had caught his words, and partly recognized him, he double-locked the door, and related to her every circumstance that had happened, and how he had managed everything; she, delighted and convinced, from the repetition of certain family secrets, known to themselves alone, embraced him, giving him as many kisses as she had bestowed tears for his death, for both were loving and tenderly attached. After reciprocal marks of each other's affection, Gabriel said to her that she must be perfectly silent, and pointed out to her how happy their life would hereafter prove; he told her of the riches he had found, and what he intended to do, the which highly delighted her. In going out, Santa pretended to cry on opening the street door, and said aloud, that she might be heard by the neighbours, " I recommend these poor fatherless children to you, signor !" To which he answered, " Fear not, good Mrs. Santa;" and walked away, full of thoughts on his future plans. When evening came on, observing the same uniform conduct of his predecessor, he went to bed, but could not sleep for thinking. No sooner did the dawn appear than he rose and went to the church of St. Catherine, where a devout and worthy pastor dwelt, and who was considered by all the Pisanians as a little Saint. Friar Angelico appearing, Gabriel told him he wanted to speak to him on particular business, and to have his advice upon a very important and singular case that had happened to him. The kind friar, although he did not know him, led him into his room.

Gabriel, who well knew the whole genealogy of Lazarus, son of Basilio of Milan, related it fully to the friar, likewise the dreadful accident, adding, that he considered himself as a principal cause of it, making him believe it was he who induced the unfortunate man to go a fishing against his will ; he represented the mischief which resulted from it to the widow and children of the deceased, and that he considered himself so much the cause of it, and felt such a weight on his conscience, that he had made up his mind, though Santa was of low condition, and poor, to take her for his wife, if she and her friends approved of it, and to take the children of the poor fisherman under his care as his own, bring them up with his own children, should he have any, and leave them coheirs with them; this, he said, would reconcile him to himself and his Maker, and be approved by men. The holy man, seeing the worthy motives which actuated him, approved of his intention, and recommended as little delay as possible, since he would thereby meet with forgiveness.

Gabriel, in order the more effectually to secure his ready co-operation, threw down thirty pieces of money, saying, that in the three succeeding Mondays he wished high mass to be sung for the soul of the deceased. At this tempting sight the friar, although a very saint, leaped with joy, took the cash, and said, " my son, the masses shall be sung next Monday; there is nothing more to attend to now but the marriage, a ceremony which I advise thee to hasten as much as thou canst; do not think of riches or noble birth ; thou art, thank heaven, rich enough; and as to birth, we are all children of one father; true nobility consists in virtue and the fear of God, nor is the good woman deficient in either; I know her well, and most of her relations." " Good father," said Gabriel, " I am come to you for the very purpose, therefore, I pray you, put me quickly in the way to forward the business."—" When will you give her the ring?" said the holy man.—" This very day," he answered, " if she be inclined."—" Well," said the friar, " go thy ways, and leave all to me; go home, and stir not from thence—these blessed nuptials shall take place." Gabriel thanked him, received his blessing, and went home.

The holy father carefully put the cash in his desk, then went to an uncle of Dame Santa, a shoemaker by trade, and a cousin of her's, a barber, and related to them what had happened; after which they went together to Dame Santa, and used every possible argument to persuade her to consent to the match, the which she feigned great difficulty in consenting to, saying that it was merely for the advantage of her children that she submitted to such a thing. I will only add, that the very same morning, by the exertions of the friar, they were married a second time; great rejoicings took place, and Gabriel and his wife laughed heartily at the simplicity of the good friar, and the credulity of the relations and neighbours. They happily lived in peace and plenty, provided for and dismissed the old servants, were blessed with two more children, whom he named *Fortunatus*, and from whom afterwards sprung some of the most renowned men, both in arms and letters.

THE RUIN OF THE ROCK; A SPANISH STORY.

> Fate sits on these dark battlements,
> And, as the portals open to receive me,
> Speaks of a nameless deed.

"LOVERS, least of all people, ought to be dilatory,"
cried Don Cavallo, yawning.—"I acknowledge it,"
returned Don Pedro; "but could I avoid the delay?
Could I help the death of the old grandee, my uncle?
And would you have had me left him and his doubloons
to disappear by themselves? I am sure you would have
thought the money at least worth looking after; and if
you had sufficient honesty, you would confess that, in
a like situation, you would have acted as I did. Then,
could I foresee that the inclemency of the weather
would force us to stop by the way? which, by the bye,
was your own proposal."—"Well, well," returned the
other, "you need say no more: for I have a notion
that we shall arrive as soon as the lady now; this
stormy weather must have delayed her as well as us.—
But I would the wind did not drive these hail-stones
against us so; they are like cannon balls, and upon the
heath will take as much effect upon us, I am afraid,
without we can find some place to retire to for shelter."
—"Travellers," interrupted Don Pedro, "must endure
all things;—for my part, I should neither care for my
own welfare or thine, could I be assured that Elvira

was in safety—but, in such hurricanes as these, the
vessel may be lost, or driven upon rocks, and the passengers perish; and with them my long-hoped-for
happiness. While such reflections haunt me, every
blast of wind strikes more forcibly to my heart than it
can possibly do to your skin."—" It will strike to my
heart too, before long," replied Cavallo, " without I can
get out of the way—would I had some strong Madeira to
keep it out ; nevertheless, I wish as much for the safety
of Elvira as yourself : St. Nicholas preserve her !—and
I would that something would preserve me, before I
am beaten to a mummy, by these plaguy hail-stones,
—could we but see an old castle now, such as we took
shelter in before."—" Wish and have," returned Don
Pedro; " if I mistake not, there is one before us.
Now I see it again, as the lightning gleams against the
battlements ; therefore let us hasten to it."

They now spurred their mules towards the place;
but a thick underwood, which surrounded the castle,
soon compelled them to alight, and pursue their way
on foot. Having fastened their mules to a stake in the
best manner that they could, they endeavoured to proceed; but, owing to the rough and uneven way, which
entangled their feet, they made but a slow progress ;
and only by the lightning could they discover that they
had not strayed from the place that they were in pursuit of. Perseverance, however, brought them to the
court yard of the castle ; and time had overthrown
many obstacles which, in the unmutilated state of the
mansion, would have opposed an effectual barrier to
their progress. " Are there any inhabitants in this

place, I wonder?" cried Don Cavallo, raising the massy knocker, "I will try." The loud and solemn report of the knocker, as it reverberated through the hollow passages of the building, impressed them with awe and dread. They waited some minutes in silence. "It is not reasonable," at length cried Don Pedro, "to suppose that this desolated ruin contains any inhabitants, unless they are pirates or plunderers, in which case we may endanger our lives by gaining admission, even if it were possible, which I think is much to be doubted."—"Hazardous or dangerous," returned Cavallo, "I am determined to make the attempt; but you may choose whether you will accompany me or not, for this dreadful weather I will not bear if I can avoid it."—"I am determined not to forsake you," replied the other; "therefore let us draw our swords and prepare for the worst that may happen." They now endeavoured to force the door, but without effect; its strength defied their united efforts, and the attempt was productive only of lassitude and fatigue. In vain they surveyed the time-worn edifice—the windows were lofty, beyond their power to reach, and secured with bars of iron; nor did there appear to be any breaches in the walls sufficiently low for them to enter by. On one side of the castle was a long terrace, which overhung the sea; from whence, when the lightning permitted, they surveyed the building with the most scrutinizing attention, but in vain; no inlet appeared, through which they could possibly effect a passage. "Would I knew that Elvira were in safety," cried Pedro sighing. "With what violence the waves dash against these walls; their hollow roaring appears to me as if it were to announce the destruction of my hopes, and I see, in imagination, the pale form of my Elvira calling on her lover to rescue her from a watery death!"—"Hold," exclaimed Cavallo, "I am sure I saw a light on the west side of the building." The light was now distinctly visible to both. Inspired with fresh hopes, they halloed as loud as possible, in hopes to gain admittance; but the loud roaring of the winds rendered the sound inaudible long before it reached that part of the building, and they were again compelled to desist from their attempts. Wearied at length with their fruitless endeavours, they resolved to return to their mules, and to try to pursue their journey in defiance of the storm; when, in hastening along the terrace, Cavalla stumbled, and, in endeavouring to recover himself, fell against a small door, hitherto concealed by a thick ivy from their view, which burst open, and precipitated him upon the floor of a room in the castle. Fortunately he received no hurt from his fall, and Pedro hastening to join him, they surveyed the apartment with mingled sensations of satisfaction and dread. It appeared to have been a private way to the terrace from the suite of apartments which occupied that side of the building. They determined to proceed; and passing through the apartment, they entered an extensive room, which seemed formerly to have been a state bedchamber. The walls were hung with tapestry, which, now damp and decayed, hung in tatters round the room; the subject was a battle of a detachment of Spaniards against a Moorish banditti; and, as they

L

passed along, the superstition which the gloom inspired seemed to give the figures animation as though they were starting from the walls to menace the intruders. The furniture and bed were fast falling to decay, and every part of the room, which displayed the most stately magnificence of former days, wore the appearance of desolation and destruction. They advanced cautiously, fearful of the sound even of their own steps, taking care to leave the doors open through which they passed, to favour their retreat in case of necessity. Light they had no means of obtaining, but the storm at times illuminated the apartments, and again plunged them into utter darkness. They now entered an anti-room, through which they passed into a grand saloon; but, like the other, its grandeur had fallen to decay. They trod lightly across it, and were preparing to pass into the next, when a violent burst from one part of the room which they were quitting, made them return as hastily as possible; but ere they gained the opposite door, a violent gust of wind, which flew along the passages, suddenly closed all the doors through which they had passed, with a tremendous noise which seemed to shake the whole fabric to its foundation. In vain did they attempt to unclose the door; it resisted their utmost efforts, and they were obliged fearfully to relinquish their design. They therefore placed themselves with a desperate resolution against it, and determined to defend themselves against their concealed enemy.

The noise still continued—Cavallo's heart sunk within him, and Don Pedro almost forgot Elvira under his present fears. It increased from the same corner of the room, and with it their alarms, till, by a violent flash of lightning, they beheld the draperies of a curtain gradually rise, after a violent flapping, and an owl flew across the apartment.

" And is this all that has frightened us ?" cried Cavallo; " I protest I thought St. Nicholas had left me to the mercy of robbers; but I am glad to find that his saintship has been more merciful."—" Do not be too sanguine," rejoined Don Pedro; " we had much difficulty to get into the castle, and we may have as much difficulty to get out again, and of the two evils I should think that much the worst; we have, therefore, nothing to do but to proceed in search of a way out, and if St. Nicholas would but guide us in this emergency, I would ever after acknowledge my obligations to him." — " Onward, then," cried Cavallo; " here is another state apartment, cousin-german to the last; but I hope it will not be found to contain such uncivil inhabitants."—" Behold another room of the same family," cried Pedro, " excepting that it is clothed differently: its garments are of cedar, you perceive."—" Yes," returned Cavallo, " and I doubt not but those pannels contain plenty of secret passages about this castle: would that we could find one that would lead us to the outside of these gloomy walls. I'll clink them, and try if they are hollow."—" Hush," cried the other, " surely I heard a noise." They listened, and with equal astonishment and horror heard, distinctly, sounds at some distance, like the screaming of one in distress, which the fear of Cavallo inter-

preted into the yells of evil spirits.—" Let us proceed,"
said Pedro, undauntedly; " this mystery shall be un-
ravelled, if human power can effect it ; come on then,
my friend, the lightning will guide us, and I am determined to follow the direction of the noise, let the
consequences be what they may."—" St. Nicholas pro-
tect us," cried Cavallo, following; " for I confess that
I feel no desire to encounter either ghosts or assassins."
With resolute courage Pedro rushed forwards, and was
followed by his more lively, yet less undaunted companion, till they reached the great entrance-hall : here
they paused, uncertain which way to pursue ; besides
the passage from which they had entered, three others
presented themselves to their view, and a grand stair-
case ; nor could they form any idea which of them
could lead to the sounds which they had so recently
heard.

. " My opinion is," cried Cavallo, " that we had
better try to walk quietly out of this door, without
setting out on a wild-goose chase we neither know
where nor for what,—perhaps after all to be frightened
by an owl again."—" I confess that I am much of
your opinion," returned Don Pedro, " so let us proceed to draw back these bolts without loss of time."
Like many other things, however, this was easier
talked of than done—the bolts and locks, rusted by
time and neglect, refused to move ; and after exhaust-
ing their united strength upon the attempt, they were
obliged to abandon it in despair.

. . " My resolution is fled," cried Cavallo; " I will
proceed no further this night, but stay here till the

morning light shall have brightened these gloomy passages."—" You may stay then by yourself," replied Pedro, " for, by St. Nicholas, this cold marble pavement chills my very heart; and, I am convinced, that to stand here another hour may be the death of us both; yet, I confess that I cannot decide how to proceed."

In vain did they endeavour to fix upon a plan for their future conduct: irresolution had deprived them of half their courage, and they stood in a state of listless anxiety, till a dismal toll on the castle bell roused them from their inactivity to a recollection of their dreadful situation. A violent noise similar to the former succeeded, but for a longer time; and the castle bell again tolled deeply, at intervals, for some minutes. With a desperate resolution they again rushed forward through one of the passages. All was silent, dark, and gloomy,—the lightning had ceased, and the moon's feeble light scarcely illumined the dusky paths which they now explored. A grated door soon arrested their farther progress, but yielded to their endeavours, and discovered a passage similar to the former. A piercing shriek, which reverberated through the echoing vaults of the ruin, fixed them horror-struck to their places— it was repeated faintly several times. Still undaunted, Pedro rushed forward, followed by his friend. Another passage succeeded — still they proceeded onwards—. and still were their souls harrowed almost to distraction by the tolling of the dreadful bell.—" As I live there is a light," cried Cavallo.—" Hush," returned the other, " tread softly." With light footsteps and

beating hearts they pursued a lambent flame, which
seemed to move along the distant extremity of the
passage; when, as they were hoping to approach it, it
suddenly disappeared, and left them in utter darkness.
Groping their way with their swords they carefully
proceeded, till the stumbling of Pedro, who was foremost, convinced them that the passage terminated in a
flight of steps.   They hesitated a few moments whether to proceed or to go back; but wonder and a strong
impulse of contending passions, determined them to
choose the former.   While descending the stairs the
shrieks were succeeded by a loud laughing, which
seemed more like the rejoicings of evil spirits than of
any human beings; but the direction from which the
sound proceeded, convinced them that they were approaching the object of their search.   The steps were
of considerable extent, but mutilated and broken, and
terminated in one of the vaults of the castle: this
vault seemed to lead to others of the same description,
and, with mingled wonder and dread, they again beheld the reflection of a light against the side of the
cavern.

They proceeded onwards to another; the light was
more distinct, and they found that it beamed through a
chasm from the adjoining cave.   Some huge masses of
rock which were strewed on the floor, enabled Don
Pedro to raise himself up so as to look into an adjoining cavern; but what could describe his terror and
astonishment, when he beheld, by the faint and uncertain light of a lamp which was suspended from the
ceiling, a newly dug grave, by the side of which was a

spade and a mattock, and a shroud lay at a small distance. While yet he gazed, the castle bell again tolled, a faintness seized him, and he was obliged to lean against the side of the cave to prevent himself from falling. Cavallo, who perceived his disorder, was in but little better condition, although he was ignorant of the cause. Again Pedro raised himself up to behold the soul-harrowing scene, which was increased by the appearance of a figure moving along in the gloom of the dungeon. The shrieks were again renewed more violently than ever, and Pedro beheld the figure glide into some more distant apartment. "I will proceed," cried he to Cavallo, "to the unravelment of this mystery, though death should follow the attempt." They retreated to another cave towards the left, and to their astonishment discovered an outlet which led to the sea beach. "St. Nicholas, be praised," cried Cavallo, "let us hasten to escape; for never did my heart jump about so at it does at this moment."—"Not so," replied the other, solemnly; "my mind is roused up to a pitch, which will not permit me to leave this place ungratified, and I cannot resolve to quit this mysterious abode, without penetrating farther: a secret impulse, which I cannot account for, impels me to the search, and it shall be made. Yet let me go alone; never shall my rashness bring my friend into danger—remain, therefore, here: and, if I live, I will return to you in half an hour."—"Wrong not my friendship so much," returned Cavallo, earnestly, "as to believe me capable of deserting you in the hour of danger. Whatever may be the perils of the enterprise, yet I am determined to share them ; nor shall persuasion induce me to rescind my resolution."—" Arm yourself with courage then," cried Pedro, advancing, " and fear nothing."

A brighter light gleamed on one side of the cave which they now entered, and they perceived an opening into the adjoining cavern. With cautious steps they crossed the vault, and placed themselves in a situation so as to observe the interior ; nor could any sight have interested their feelings in a higher degree than the one which they now beheld. A lady on her knees before two ruffians, seemed to implore their pity. " I have already given you all that I am possessed of," cried she, in supplicating accents, " I have no more."—" We know it, pretty lady," returned one of the villains, " but we must not leave you the power to hang us for our plunder—fortune seldom sends us such a booty, and we must guard against even possibilities, and not stand the chance of having it taken away from us again : you must, therefore, prepare to die—the grave is already dug, the bell has been tolled to answer a double purpose (since it would be sure to deter every one from approaching the place), and a shroud is ready at hand, so that you will have the satisfaction of being buried in a decent manner."—" And have you then saved me from a watery grave," continued the lady, " to murder me on shore ? Better that I had perished with my companions, and that the sea had received me, than to be preserved only to die a more cruel death by the hands of ruffians." — " We should have got nothing by that though," cried the villain ; " but come, we have no time for parleying, so prepare for death. Sancho, count out those ducats, while I sharpen this sword a bit."——"Oh! Pedro, Pedro," cried the lady, with streaming eyes, "where are you now?"——"Who?" cried the ruffian, tearing off her veil.——"Heavens! 'tis Elvira herself," cried Don Pedro, rushing forward, and springing upon the ruffian, while Cavallo at the same moment seized the other, and after a long struggle, as the ruffian was unarmed, succeeded in fastening him to the wall so effectually, as to deprive him of all farther exertion, with some ropes which were lying on the ground. He then hastened to the assistance of Don Pedro, who maintained an obstinate battle with the other; and in consequence of his opponent being well armed, and desperate with rage and disappointment, had to support a skilful attack, which might have terminated fatally, had not the assassin's sword breaking, laid him at the mercy of the conqueror.——"And is it Pedro then," cried Elvira, "who has thus rescued me! what fatality directed thee so opportunely to my assistance? O, my good Cavallo too! But say what chance can have conducted you to this dreary abode?"—— "You shall know all," cried Don Pedro, and proceeded thus . . . .

EDELIZA; A TALE OF THE FRENCH COURT.

"Nothing is so glorious in the eyes of mankind, and ornamental to human nature, setting aside the infinite advantages which arise from it, as a strong, steady, masculine piety; but enthusiasm and superstition are the weakness of human reason, that expose us to the scorn and derision of infidels, and sink us even below the beasts that perish."—SPECTATOR.

EDELIZA, the orphan daughter of Albert De Liera-mont, passed her early years, secluded from the world, in an old chateau on the banks of the Garonne. Here her days rolled on in uninterrupted quiet, and the native cheerfulness of her mind was unbroken by care. Though deprived of her mother a few moments after she first beheld the light, and of her father ere she had learned to lisp his name, the infant years of Edeliza were cherished with tenderness by the Duke of ****, to whom De Lieramont, with his dying breath, had bequeathed her, together with a small sum of money, the only remains of his large property, which he had dissipated in his zeal to support the protestant interest. The duke had been the early patron of De Lieramont, with him had embraced the reformation, and borne arms in defence of his principles. The enfeebled state of this nobleman's health rendering him incapable of supporting the fatigues of public life, he retired, soon after Edeliza became an inmate of his family, from the turbulent scenes this period exhibited, to the peaceful shades of his well fortified chateau. The duke, from whose marriage no progeny had issued, and whose wife possessed few qualities to interest his heart, soon felt for the young orphan the tenderest regard; and the care of her education became the employment and solace of his declining years.

The guardian of Edeliza possessed a warm imagination and a feeling heart; but the powers of his mind were contracted by prejudice, and his judgment was weak almost to infantine puerility. The heart of the little orphan was formed for love; and her guardian, by insensible degrees, became the object of her warmest affections. Her reverence for his opinions was almost idolatrous, and she relied on his judgment with implicit confidence. Lessons of religion were the first which her zealous instructor endeavoured to impress on the ductile mind of his pupil, and devotional feelings mingled with the earliest ideas which her mind imbibed. Yet she contemplated a Deity she could not comprehend. As her guardian, heated by the zeal of a sectary, described him, he appeared to her unsophisticated mind a being actuated by revenge, delighting in the destruction of his creatures, and she shrunk with horror from the picture imagination presented. But when she gazed on the face of nature, a warmer sentiment pervaded her heart. The earth teeming with varied existence, the vegetable tribe rich in beauty, and the animal creation sporting over the meadows, or filling the air with harmony, roused her soul to transport, and her mind rose with grateful rapture to the stupendous cause of being.

As Edeliza was allowed to wander without restraint
over the beautiful scenery that surrounded the chateau,
her mind gained, by contemplating those interesting
objects, a degree of strength which the education of the
duke was ill calculated to bestow.   These scenes roused
her morbid faculties, and awakened the germ of intellect; but they likewise contributed to inflame her
youthful imagination, and excite her sensibility.

Influenced by this desultory mode of education, she
attained the season of womanhood with a mind weak-
ened by superstition and enslaved by fear, though it
was not wholly devoid of energy; and there were
moments when her understanding rose superior to prejudice.   Her heart was warmly susceptible of pleasure
and pain; and her passions, though yet unawakened,
were kindled with ardour.   It was in vain that the pursuit of knowledge was forbidden to Edeliza, that the
spirit of youthful inquiry was repressed by the chilling
influence of superstition : her heart panted to embrace
a wider circle : and, as her reason matured, an ardent
wish to wander from the environs of the chateau banished content from her breast.

The hour at length arrived which was to gratify this
craving curiosity.   The party, of which the duke was
still considered a chief, began to tremble for its safety.
Henry the Fourth of France had renounced the protestant faith, and distraction seemed ready to overwhelm
them.   The expansive and philosophic mind of this
monarch was but little understood by the religious bigots
of those times ; they could not enter into his schemes,
nor comprehend the benevolence that dictated his actions.

The guardian of Edeliza was roused by the perils to which his party seemed exposed ; and forgetting, in the ardour of his zeal, the infirmities of his age, he resolved to appear once more on the theatre of the world. With a light heart did the young orphan, who was now too dear to be left behind, bid adieu to the scenes of her infancy. A crowd of new and delightful emotions filled her heart, as they journeyed, by slow stages, to the court of France. A quick succession of ideas passed rapidly through her mind, which seemed to open on a new existence; to imbibe " food for contemplation even to madness." The charms of Edeliza, when aided by the force of novelty, were too powerful to pass unnoticed even amidst the beauties of a court; while the native simplicity of her manners, and the vigour of her imagination, gave a grace to her person irresistably fascinating. She was presently surrounded by admirers ; and, intoxicated with the new delight, her heart yielded to the allurements of vanity. Each day she passed amidst varied scenes of dissipation, and each night she wept with fruitless regret and unavailing penitence, the follies of the day: for a life so opposite to her former habits, so repugnant to her ideas of duty, could not be embraced without a strong mixture of pain. But her understanding, deprived by education of firmness, was unable to resist, the impetuosity of her senses imperiously demanding gratification, and she was condemned to experience the alternate feelings of eager delight and bitter remorse. A new and unexpected scene was, however, preparing for Edeliza ; a scene calculated to call forth all the enthusiasm

of her temper, and awaken the warm affections of her
heart.

The eyes of the monarch had dwelt with delight on
the charms of the young orphan, from the first moment
the duke had presented this cherished object to the
gaze of his sovereign; and admiration, in the susceptible heart of Henry, was soon kindled into love.   In
the society of young Edeliza he forgot the cares of
state, the turbulence of faction, and the fatigues of
war.   It was peculiarly soothing to a mind like his,
disgusted with the bigotry of contending parties, and
wearied with unavailing struggles, to listen to her un-
tutored ideas, to observe the wild and energetic bursts
of feeling and intellect which education had not been
able wholly to suppress.   Every moment that the enraptured monarch could disengage from the calls of
business were spent in her apartments, and this growing
intercourse served to rivet more strongly the fetters
that bound him.   Edeliza contemplated the expanded
mind of the prince with wonder and delight; it was to
her a new source of intelligence; a field in which her
fancy could incessantly wander, and find fresh food for
the awakened intellect to feed on.   His attentions, too,
flattered her pride, excited self-approbation, and
soothed the feelings of her heart, which panted for
some object on whom to lavish its vast stores of affection, and her passion soon became more ardent than
his own.   It was in vain that her judgment represented
the danger of such unequal attachments; for, though
her mind would have shrunk from any act injurious
to virtue, yet to love a monarch, the father of his

people, seemed a sentiment which no rigour could condemn: brought up in ignorance of the world and its laws, they had little influence in forming her opinions.

The attachment of the prince to the young stranger could not long remain a secret; and the protestants flattered themselves that they should, by her means, gain a complete ascendance over the mind of their sovereign, while the catholics trembled at the power of an unlettered girl. But the hopes and fears of each party gave to her an influence she was far from possessing. The actions of this prince were generally formed by the dictates of his understanding, not directed by the caprice of his favourites: he was too just, too benevolent, to consent, in an hour of dalliance, to an act that might deluge a whole province in blood.

Thus did Edeliza, scarce conscious of her elevation, become the rising sun before whom the satellites of a court paid their daily adorations: thus, too, held up to the shafts of envy, and marked as the object of suspicion, she became the victim of those who trembled at her power. The few minutes daily passed in the society of her lover, were imbued with delight too exquisite to be interrupted by political squabbles, and months had passed away before Edeliza could find an opportunity of pleading the protestant cause with the enraptured Henry, though repeatedly urged to the undertaking by the duke and his party. She at length entered on the subject with that warmth of feeling which characterized all her actions. The early impressions her fancy had received rushed on her heart, and gave eloquence to her tongue ; and she became at once the zealous advocate of a cause which all her habits had taught her to reverence. Henry listened with delight to her persuasive language, while he gazed with rapture on the charms of her person, heightened by elevated feelings ; but when she had finished, assuming a severer tone than he had ever yet addressed her in, he replied—

" Edeliza, I regard the cause for which you now plead with reverence, because I know it is calculated to enlighten mankind. Religious dissensions have already roused the spirit of inquiry, and will, by slow degrees, spread knowledge over the world. Inquiry kindles the dormant faculties of the human mind, and before awakened intellect, misery and barbarism must vanish from the earth. But my conduct, on the present occasion, must be left to my own judgment : I will not allow you to be the tool of a party, nor myself to be biassed by feeling ; therefore, on this subject, I will never listen to you more. Farewell, my love !—for the present we must part."

Edeliza was chagrined by the harshness of her lover; but a spark of latent vanity, which circumstances conspired to foster, prevented her acknowledging, even to the duke, the ill success of her mission; and some privileges granted to the protestants shortly after this period, though resulting from the monarch's judgment, were attributed to her influence.

The party began now to exult ; they fancied they had found in Edeliza a proper instrument to bind the prince to their interest. They calculated on the warm feelings of Henry, aided by his natural propensity to love; and every art was practised to increase his infatuation, and place his victim more completely in his power. Time passed with Edeliza in a round of delight. Henry loved her with the most fervent passion; but the native generosity of his mind had hitherto prevented his requesting any favour inconsistent with her own ideas of virtue. She was the orphan daughter of De Lieramont, an officer who had toiled in his affairs and bled in his service; and could a heart imbued with the principles of justice, repay the activity of a departed friend by the dishonour of his child?——No! the judgment of Henry shrunk from the action; though his fevered imagination dwelt incessantly on the accomplishment of his wishes. But the life of this monarch was not destined to be long stationary, and some convulsions in a distant province soon drew him from this scene of temptation: the danger which called for his presence was urgent, and the prince had but a few hours to prepare for his departure. To bid adieu to Edeliza was reserved as his last care; it was a task at once painful and pleasing, and he wished the parting words of her he loved to rest on his mind undissipated by vulgar objects. It was midnight when he entered her apartment: she received him with trembling emotion, oppressed by contending feelings——she wept on his bosom, while her heart beat with a painful presentiment of impending evil——she dreaded to hear the last farewell of her lover, for her disordered fancy foreboded it would be an eternal adieu. In vain he at-

M

tempted to calm her agitated mind—in vain he urged
all that reason could suggest to quiet her fears ; but in
vain the soothing accents of love flowed from his lips :
the dawn summoned the monarch away, and left Edeliza a prey to the most tormenting anxiety. Alas! she
was not only a prey to corroding sorrow : the engines
of malice were at work for her destruction, and the
absence of her lover seemed a favourable opportunity
of employing their force. The duke, her only protector, was lulled into a fatal security: he judged that,
elevated as she now was, no one would have the teme-
rity to attack her, and various schemes were formed
for removing her from the court without exciting her
suspicions.

How changed was the scene to the hapless orphan!
No allurements could draw her from her melancholy
contemplations : the dissipation that surrounded her
had lost its power to charm. Her only amusement
now was to sing her complaints to the strains of her
lute, in the simple language her feelings dictated. It
had been her custom since the departure of Henry, to
linger away the long summer evenings in a little hermitage on the summit of a hill, from whose height an
artificial torrent fell into a lake below. Here she indulged in visions of fancy : and here her mind, glowing with the mingled feelings of love and devotion,
rose to a degree of sublimity almost above mortality.
Fears for the safety of her lover shook her soul : all
around her was darkness and suspense, and her heart
fondly clung to the Invisible Spirit whose power moves
the planets in their orbits, for support and protec-

tion. While in this gloomy cell, her lips poured forth to Deity all the tender wishes that warmed her throbbing bosom.

It was after an evening of more than usual gloom in the mind of Edeliza, when, returning through the long avenue of trees that led to her apartments, her ears were struck with the sound of distant music. The night was sultry, not a breeze moved through the ripened foliage, and the harmony of the feathered choir was hushed in silence. It seemed like a pause in creation; and the soft sounds that now floated in the air appeared, to her heated imagination, like the voice of some invisible spirit. She stopped to listen; while the mingled emotions of surprize, admiration, and terror, played about her heart. The sounds, though distant, were clear; and she distinctly heard the following words, sung in tones the most impressive, by a voice whose melting softness stole upon the enraptured ear—

> " Haste, fond victim of love's power !
> Haste, ere yet the destined hour
> Dooms thee to the snare.''

Edeliza trembled: a crowd of indistinct ideas rushed upon her mind, while a thousand vague fears filled her fancy. The words seemed addressed to her, and the time and place gave them double force. But whither was she to haste? From what snare was she to fly? Who had formed the thought of injuring her? And why this mysterious address?

The music ceased, and again profound silence reigned;

Edeliza raised her eyes fearfully from the ground, as she cautiously proceeded on her way. The moon-beams shone faintly through the lofty trees, and shed an indistinct light over the path, which, by discovering objects without developing their form, served but to increase the gloom. With trembling and irresolute steps she moved forward, when the solemn silence was again interrupted by a noise like the clanking of chains, which seemed slowly advancing towards her. She paused with increased emotion, when a sudden light discovered to her view an object whose terrific appearance almost shook reason from her seat. Fear palsied her soul: she sank on her knees, and vainly endeavoured to implore the protection of Heaven; but her lips were locked in silence, while terror bound up her faculties, and seemed to chain her to the spot. The figure at length approached; and, stretching his arm to raise her from the ground, she again looked fearfully up, and beheld, with frantic terror, the being before her. It bore the form of an aged warrior, whose hoary beard hung below his breast, and shaded the glittering steel that enveloped his body. A helmet covered his forehead, round which a phosphoric flame played, and gave a livid hue to his countenance, in which time and deep thought had left strong traces. To his left arm was fastened a chain, and in his right he held a sceptre of livid fire.

After a pause of inexpressible terror, the apparition, in a voice which appeared to issue from the ground, thus addressed her :

" Fair daughter of this lower world, thy piety hath

ascended to heaven, and thy zeal, though mistaken, shall be rewarded. Thou hast strayed in the paths of perdition, and I am sent to snatch thee from destruction. Follow me to where peace and happiness await thee, where roses shall spring in thy path, and where the thorns of life never wound. Eternal bliss shall be the reward of thy temporal obedience. But dare to dispute my mandate, and I have power to hurl thee to the lowest gulf of wretchedness, where lingering despair shall canker thy soul, and hopeless anguish prey on thy vitals.

As the spectre finished these words, he threw round her the chain; which fastening again to his arm with a spring, he drew her along with an impetuosity which her trembling and enfeebled limbs could scarcely support. At length they entered, beneath a broken arch, the ruin of a gothic chapel. Here they paused; and Edeliza, casting an imploring look on her conductor, raised her clasped hands to heaven; while she besought his compassion in language wild and incoherent as were the feelings of her mind. But her efforts were soon chilled by new terrors: the solid ground on which she stood shook beneath her feet, while a hoarse discordant noise seemed to fill the distant cavities, whose mouldering ruins tottered beneath the mighty crash. She now beheld, by the light of the flaming sceptre, which her companion waved along the earth, a wide chasm, down the broken steps of which he again impelled her unwilling feet. As they entered the vault beneath, Edeliza gazed fearfully round; a phosphoric flame blazed round the pillars that supported the broken arches, from which, in beautiful variety, hung innumerable forms of crystalline spar, transparent as the dew-drop in the rays of morning, and glittering with the faint light that filled the cavern.   The scene was at once sublime and terrible; but the mind of Edeliza was awake only to sensations of horror, and she uttered a loud and piercing shriek, as the strong arm of her mysterious guide drew her forcibly along the subterraneous passage. They had not, however, proceeded far, when the light from the pillars was suddenly extinguished, the blazing sceptre vanished from the hand of her conductor, and the bright flame that played round his helmet expired.   Edeliza became frantic with affright, and a happy insensibility benumbed her powers.   In this state she was conveyed to the convent of ———, against whose gloomy walls the waves beat with a monotonous sadness, which seemed to proclaim the tedious uniformity that characterised the lives of its pensive inhabitants.

While these dark scenes were acting beneath the bosom of the earth, the friends of Edeliza became a prey to the most anxious solicitude.   With fruitless inquietude did they explore the hermitage, and wander over the spacious gardens; the object of their search was nowhere to be found.   The ladies who had attended on the hapless stranger since her arrival at court, were alarmed through the night with incessant forebodings. At one moment the tapestry that decorated the apartments was shaken as with a strong eddy, while deep and hollow groans seemed to issue from the uncouth figures; and twice, when all else was silent, an unknown voice was heard to pronounce these words:

" Go not to the aid of De Lieramont's daughter: the measure of her crimes is now full, and she must receive the reward of her guilt."

The night passed in fearful consternation and suspense! but, as the dawn again brightened the atmosphere, the duke, with renovated hopes, renewed the search. His labours and solicitude were now soon ended; for, on again entering the hermitage, a small door was discovered, which had hitherto escaped observation. The companions of the duke eagerly entered the aperture; while he, with feeble and hesitating steps, followed to witness a catastrophe more terrible than even his fears had suggested.

Stretched on the ground, in one corner of the apartment, lay a corpse, clad in the garments of the blooming Edeliza. The duke gazed on the form before him: it was the figure of the being most dear to his heart: but so changed was the countenance, where yesterday hope and animation beamed; so distorted were the features by the convulsive agonies of death, that not a trace remained which could recall her image to his memory. Yet he could not for a moment sooth his lacerated bosom with hope: the lifeless figure bore an exact resemblance to that of his beloved orphan; and his heart sickened at the thought, that here she had perished without one friend to soothe the last agonies of expiring nature. Sunk in profound melancholy, he was led by his friends from this oppressive scene: but all their efforts to divert his grief were ineffectual ; he had lost in Edeliza the last prop on which his affections hung, and despair withered the little energy that yet remained to support his enfeebled frame.

The body was conveyed to the palace, and in a few days consigned to the tomb with all the pomp of ostentatious sorrow. The story of Edeliza's death filled the city with astonishment, and engrossed the attention of all ranks in society. The strange and unnatural noises which were said to have predicted her dissolution ; the figure with the burning helmet, who had been seen the preceding evening in the garden—and fancy had given to it a thousand different shapes—all these were circumstances of such strong import, as to induce a belief of supernatural agency ; and so strong was the force of opinion, that even the wise and reflective were borne down with the general current. A belief in miracles has been in all ages the refuge of weak and ignorant minds : it belongs to the scholar and philosopher to detect error, to trace causes from effects, and to bring fraud and imposition to light ; but no such, alas ! were at hand to rescue an hapless stranger, and Edeliza soon sunk into oblivion, forgotten by the world around. The monarch received the tidings of her death at a time when calamity seemed to overwhelm his mighty mind. He had just lost a battle—had witnessed the horrors of an ensanguined field—had seen numbers of his subjects fall beneath the destroying sword—and existence appeared scarce worth the constant toil that preserved it. The heart of Henry was formed for the most ardent feelings : he loved Edeliza with passionate fondness, and this new sorrow, for a time, sunk him in despair. He shut himself in his tent, where for several days none of his courtiers dared to intrude, and neglecting all business, he was wholly occupied by despair. Necessity at length aroused him from this lethargic sadness; and, once awakened to the calls of duty, he soon forgot, in the exertions of the monarch, the afflictions of the man. He had no doubt but the death of Edeliza had been caused by some sudden attack of disease, which for want of immediate assistance had proved fatal. The stories that were told him of the miracles which announced her dissolution, he laughed at as the superstitions of the idle crowd, and they left no trace on his mind.

While thus lamented by her lover, as in opinion he consigned her to an early grave, Edeliza was slowly recovering from the shock her reason had sustained, within the gloomy walls of a convent, destined to be her living tomb. It was many weeks before she recovered recollection; and when she did, images of the past floated so confusedly over her mind, that her whole life seemed to have been but a lengthened dream of existence. Her memory bore only faint traces of the night when she had been hurried away from a spot dear to her heart : and so forcibly were the impressions of infancy fastened on her mind, that she gave a ready ear to the tales of those around her. Superstitious terrors were the first impressions she had received ; and she listened with horror to the incredible account of her having been brought to her present abode in the dead of night, without human agency, amidst the howling of winds, the crash of thunders, and the blaze of elemental fires.   Alas, in how many ways does vanity mislead its votaries !   For, had the judgment of Edeliza been unbiassed, she could not have believed this ridiculous story ; could never have supposed, that for an atom like herself the operations of nature would have been suspended.   Imbued with such feelings, it was, however, no difficult task to persuade her that the tenets of her former creed were the tenets of error.   She shuddered at the thought of a justly incensed God taking vengeance of her crimes, and her heart glowed with pious rapture for the mercy that had snatched her from destruction.   Most willingly did she embrace the catholic faith, and most willingly did she perform the penances enjoined for her past errors.   Yet, as she counted her beads with tears and remorse, the image of her beloved Henry stole over her thoughts, and the remembrance of him mingled with her most ardent prayers to the throne of beneficence.   Corroded by the vain desires of ungratified passion, which solitude and religious fervour heightened almost to madness, Edeliza passed her melancholy days, while the sallow hue of disappointment withered the roses in her cheeks, and blasted the fair form of beauty.   Yet the heroism which disappointed love inspired, elevated her soul, and gave to her gloomy abode a secret charm. · There were moments in which she doubted the propriety of her conduct, and feared she had been too hasty in her judgment : but the mingled sensations of love and piety soon checked the suggestions of reason ; and, hurried away by the enthusiasm of her character, she became, as life declined, the most rigid recluse of a severe order.

The abbé ———, by whose artifices she had been spirited away, rejoiced in his machinations. He was the spectre who had conducted her through the subterraneous passage, and then, consigning her to the care of a trusty agent, returned to manage the concluding scene. He had previously procured the body of a peasant girl, whose countenance, distorted by the strong convulsions in which she had expired, bore no trace of any living object ; and, having dressed it in the clothes of his unfortunate victim, and secretly conveyed it to her favourite haunt, wisely trusted to the superstition of those around him to aid and give complete success to the deceit.

His plot succeeded even beyond his expectations, and many years after he boasted of having, by a little deception, rescued an amiable woman from perdition, and saved his monarch from the fascination of her charms.

THE THREE BEAUTIES OF DRESDEN.

Beauties, in vain, their pretty eyes may roll,
Charms strike the sight,—but merit wins the soul.

THE troops of the Elector of Saxony were repairing to winter quarters, after a tedious but, at length, successful campaign against Frederic the Great. The capital had very lately been threatened with a siege by the Prussian monarch, and it was principally owing to the excellent conduct and astonishing intrepidity of a regiment of dragoons, that the late desperate engagement had terminated in favour of the Electorate. They turned the tide of fortune: the Saxon army, which had been very nearly discomfited, rallied when they beheld the glorious stand made by these brave men, and inspired by their example, they rushed upon the enemy, and obliged him, beaten at all points, not only to quit the field, but to relinquish, for the present at least, his ambitious designs, and his intended attempt upon the capital. A truce was asked and obtained, and the remains of those gallant hussars, who had so gloriously distinguished themselves, galloped into Dresden upon a bright morning in the beginning of December. In addition to their own victorious standards, they brought with them the eagle of Prussia, wrested from the king's immediate guard, and with trumpets sounding and banners flying, they proceeded along the principal

streets to the grand square. Shouts and acclamations attended them in their progress through the city, and every window and every balcony were filled with beauties eager to reward the exertions of valour with their smiles. Victor Amadeus Wallenstein, a young man of seven-and-twenty, who had been raised to the rank of colonel by his almost marvellous achievements, was the chief object of attraction. His bravery scarcely equalled his beauty, and he managed his prancing steed with so much grace, that the whole city rang with the praises of his person and accomplishments. It was a proud and happy moment for the fearless soldier; he had escaped disease or wounds in many severe hardships and well-contested fields; and after a life of toil and danger, and banishment from social intercourse with the fairer portion of the world, he was going to spend a whole season in a festive city, with a name that ensured him a general welcome. Wallenstein speedily experienced the hospitality of the inhabitants; no ball or party was considered to be complete without the handsome Colonel; and he entered into the amusements of the place with the avidity of a young and sanguine heart, secure of finding the pleasure which he sought. To fall in love was a matter of course, and though for some time puzzled how to choose amid so many beauties, a slight sentiment of vanity decided him. Romilda Blumenberg, a lady of high birth, was the star of the Electoral court; all the gay and noble of the city paid homage to her charms. She was somewhat capricious and difficult of

access; which, in the opinion of many, enhanced the
value of the rare and brilliant smiles she sometimes
condescended to bestow.

Wallenstein had been early struck with the commanding character of her fine features; he saw that she
extended even the common courtesies of life but to
few, and attributing the haughty demeanour, which
gained her numerous enemies, to a dignified reserve
which shrank from the freedoms that others permitted
without scruple, he began to feel a restless desire to
thaw the ice of this lovely yet frigid maiden.   The
gallant Colonel was not formed to sue long in vain :
his paternal estate was large, and the favour which he
so justly enjoyed at court, seemed to promise promotion to the highest ranks of his profession.   In point
of birth, fortune, and expectations, therefore, he might
be deemed a fitting match for any lady below the dignity of a royal descent; and with the addition of his
superior personal advantages, there could be little
doubt of his success.   Romilda, even at first elated by
this new conquest beyond the usual cold satisfaction
with which she was wont to regard a fresh accession to
her train, forbore the practice of those disdainful airs,
so chilling to the hopes of her less favoured lovers;
she received Wallenstein with a sweet graciousness,
which convinced him he was not mistaken in supposing
that she possessed a heart fraught with the most
amiable and tender emotions.   He became every day
more and more enamoured, as new perfections deve-
loped themselves; and this fair, yet hitherto cold-

bosomed creature, seemed to melt by degrees, until she returned his fond devotion with an equal sincerity of affection.

The triumph which Colonel Wallenstein had obtained over many titled suitors, afforded a theme of conversation to the idle portion of the community ; the rejected and their friends were not sparing in their sneers and animadversions upon the subject ; and a particular party, who generally assembled at a palace inhabited by Prince Albert of Saxe Saalfeldt, then resident, upon a mission of great importance, at Dresden, were the most bitter in their indignation, at the success of a man who had already raised their envy by the fame which rewarded his martial exploits. Prince Albert had numerous reasons for disliking the accomplished soldier. He had once, even at the outset of Wallenstein's military service, been worsted by him in a skirmish ; and since his arrival in the capital, he had been severely mortified by his steady refusal to join the loud and licentious revels which he was in the habit of holding in his saloons. Victor, disgusted with scenes of drunkenness and riot, had wholly withdrawn himself from the society of the Prince, who, following the bent of a fickle humour, was now running a wild career of dissipation. Never seen in assemblies frequented by the virtuous of either sex, he drained the midnight bowl with companions of the same caste ; yet, gifted with considerable talent, and often emerging from a life degraded by vice, he was not condemned as incorrigibly devoted to reprobate habits. His exalted station procured him many friends, who prophesied

that he would live to redeem the errors of his youth;
and the strong necessity in the existing state of Saxony
to conciliate the imperial family, with whom he was
allied, rendered the court and cabinet anxious to pal-
liate, to overlook, and to excuse excesses, which in
others would have been visited with the strongest cen-
sure.   Though the Prince had for a long time ceased
to attend the entertainments given by the nobility, he
still retained a lively recollection of the charms of
Romilda Blumenberg, and regularly paid the doubtful
compliment of pronouncing her name before his ablu-
tions, in union with the most base and worthless females of the city : and when Wallenstein's reported
engagement was announced to him, he exclaimed with
a deep oath, that the milk-sop was not worthy of the
fairest hand in Dresden.   " Ye have done wrong, gal-
lants," he continued, " to allow this gunpowder hero
to mingle myrtles with his laurels : by the red lip of
St. Catherine, I will overcome my constitutional lazi-
ness, meet him in the field of love, and snatch away
the prize.   What say you, friends ? I'll wager a thousand ducats, and the best barb in my stable to boot,
that I oblige Wallenstein to retreat."   The bet was
immediately accepted, and the Prince offered fresh
stakes—his jewels to one, his pictures to another, and
lastly his plate : they were eagerly taken, for Wallenstein's marriage appeared to be certain, and the chances
were very strongly in favour of Albert's forgetfulness
of the whole affair.   The news, however, was buzzed
about the city the next day; Victor heard it, but it
did not cause any uneasiness in him: it was brought to

the toilette of the lady, and she was highly indignant at Prince Albert's presumptuous hopes. To the surprise of many, he appeared that evening at a ball. Romilda displayed her resentment by the most contemptuous neglect. He yielded to none in the grace and dignity of his deportment—there was no possibility of repulsing his easy assurance; and, undaunted by her disdainful glances, he remained her shadow for the whole evening.

Wallenstein would have been better pleased had Romilda treated the Prince with quiet indifference; but the error was of the judgment only, and he would not pain his fair friend by remarking it. The next morning he found her laughing over some very fine verses which she had just received; she tore them in his presence, and flung them into the fire. At night the Prince was at his post again, and occasionally extracted a word from the lady, fairly tired, it should seem, of her impenetrability. Wallenstein still would not allow himself to feel uncomfortable; but though, on the following day, he was almost certain that he saw Albert's page in the palace-yard, he was not shewn any more letters, and in the evening Romilda was both thoughtful and languid in the dance; and when, complaining of fatigue, she sat down, the Prince was allowed to lean over the back of her chair, and to make as many fine speeches as he pleased.

The Colonel now began to experience some uneasy sensations. So long as Romilda had checked the advances of this insolent suitor, for her sake he was disposed to overlook the liberty which he had taken with

N

her name; but he now determined upon shewing his resentment upon the first fitting opportunity.   Watching their conduct closely, he saw that Romilda was dazzled by the splendour of her supposed conquest: stung to the quick, he left her to the blandishments to which she lent so willing an ear; yet, unable to seek his pillow, he wandered around the residence of his beloved for several hours.

Towards morning, the light of a waning moon revealed the figure of a man leaping the garden wall : Wallenstein darted forward—it was the Prince ! Instantly drawing his sword, he commanded him to defend himself.   Albert, with cool imperturbility, called the guard, and in another moment the challenger was deprived of his sword, and placed in close custody.   Many days elapsed ere Wallenstein was released, and it required all his own interest, and the strongest exertions on the part of his friends, to procure his pardon;   the laws against duelling were exceedingly severe, and had not Prince Albert interceded with the Elector, they would probably have been enforced.   The Prince gave himself infinite credit for his forbearance, since, had the combat actually taken place, Wallenstein must have been sentenced to banishment at the least, a punishment little less than that which he endured in owing his security to the man who had so deeply mortified him.

Romilda's share in the mal-accident obliged her to retire from court ; the Prince, having won his bets, pursued her no more; and Victor, ashamed of his attachment to one so heartless, strove to divert his mind by new scenes and new amusements. The burghers of Dresden, eager to shew their high esteem of Colonel Wallenstein, had prepared for him a magnificent present, consisting of the precious manufacture of the city, the rich china so highly celebrated throughout Europe: a deputation waited upon him, to invite him to the house of one of the principal merchants, where he found the chief citizens assembled, together with their wives and daughters. Victor lent apparent attention to the long-winded orations and laboured compliments, delivered with considerable difficulty by the civic authorities, whilst his eyes glanced over the fair faces of the damsels, who, shrinking behind their mothers, blushed deeply at his regards: there was one who far exceeded her companions in beauty and grace; her cheeks were suffused with a richer crimson, and her eyes flashed out brighter beams when those of the gallant Colonel rested upon her glowing countenance. The first ceremonial over, this young creature, though evidently embarrassed by her timidity, advanced a few paces, and having singled out six of the youngest and prettiest in the company, who arranged themselves into a group, motioned them to follow her as she stepped forward, and, with downcast looks and hesitating accents, approached the hero of the day.

"Alas!" said she, "I have forgotten my speech; but I am directed to tell you, sir, that the women of Dresden are not ungrateful to the patriot-band who saved the city from the horrors of a siege; and, though most unworthy of your acceptance, they entreat that you will accept this vase from their hands. We do not pretend to vie with our fathers and brothers in the gift; but we trust that as it has been purchased by the product of our industry, exerted for the purpose, you will not disdain so trifling a record of our deep sense of your merits."

Wallenstein made a suitable reply, and his polite gallantry increased the favourable impression which he had made upon the assembly. A magnificent collation was now set out, which afforded him an opportunity of giving a bright example to the male part of the company by his unceasing attentions to the ladies. When the repast was concluded, a band of music commenced a popular air, and Victor instantly led Ernestine Vanhagen to the dance. The evening passed delightfully away; his fair partner was all innocence and simplicity, and, unacquainted with the arts of her sex, took no pains to disguise her admiration of the handsome hussar. What a contrast to Romilda; and how much more attractive was such frank sincerity, than the cold and studied airs of that calculating coquette!

Wallenstein's style of living was almost entirely changed : he went seldom to court, but amused himself with domestic parties given by the honest burgesses. Ernestine led him to her favourite walks round the city ; she displayed a charming taste for the beauties of nature, as they wandered under the spreading pine-trees which crown the rocky banks of the sparkling Elbe ; and whilst standing together in the cupola of the Frauenkirche, she pointed out to him the distant hills Der Tacchishen Schweitz, and described to him her own pleasant dairy in that romantic region, he thought that he could relinquish all the glories of his profession, to lead a pastoral life with so sweet a companion. In fact, the prejudices of aristocracy were melting fast away, and Victor, too honourable to win a maiden's heart, and leave her to weep over his desertion, had determined to raise the burgher's daughter to the rank of his wife.

The birth-day of the Elector occurred in this month, and was celebrated with great magnificence: there was a masked ball at court, and a sort of carnival established throughout the city; all ranks and classes appearing in the streets and public places in fanciful dresses. Victor was engaged to meet Ernestine at the house of a friend. After he had paid his respects to his sovereign, disengaging himself as quickly as possible from the brilliant assembly, he hastened to his appointment. The streets were blazing with torches and ringing with minstrelsy; as he passed along, group after group, in quaint disguises, accosted him with many speeches, and the spirit of joy seemed to be abroad. He hurried forward to make his lovely friend a sharer in the universal gaiety; but she was not to be found. Vainly did he search the houses of their mutual acquaintance, all those which were open for the reception of masks he had visited save one—it was Prince Albert's. It was splendidly lighted, and music sounded from within: he hesitated, yet entered. The Prince, superbly dressed, was parading the principal apartment unmasked; a lady, covered with a flowing veil, leaned upon his arm; the height, the air, was that of Ernestine! Victor gazed for a moment in doubt and dismay; he pulled off his hat and mask for air, and in another moment caught the regards of the veiled female—she uttered a faint shriek—his fears were verified; and hastening up to her, he exclaimed, " Have you been betrayed into this den of vice, or did you enter it with your own consent ?"

Her whole frame shook with the conflict of her feelings—her veil fell aside, and disclosed a face quivering with agitation. Wallenstein grasped his sword; but, clasping her hands together, and rushing forward to prevent the rash design, she said, " Do not hazard your life for one so unworthy. I came here by my own consent."

Victor turned away; but he could not leave without an effort to save her from farther wretchedness and degradation—" Return with me, at least, to your parents," he cried.

" Oh! no, no, no !" she replied, wrapping up her head in her veil, " never shall I behold either them or you again."

All this time the Prince stood silently by, with a calm, cold look : his easy indifference roused Wallenstein to desperation—fire flashed from his eyes; and having drawn his sword, he menaced him with a blow; but Ernestine perceiving the action even through her veil, threw herself into Albert's arms, and Victor, dropping his weapon, rushed out of the palace.

Every feeling of Wallenstein's heart was outraged; his pride and his affection were equally wounded. Scarcely able to restrain the passionate impulse which prompted him to take a deep and speedy revenge upon the base contriver of his wretchedness, he wildly resolved to crush him like a noisome reptile, or hunt him as a beast of prey; but reflection, in bringing even more bitter mortification, turned the tide of his thoughts. Ernestine's confession cut him to the soul; should he forfeit his life and honour for a creature so easily won.

Wallenstein was seen no more in the haunts of the gay; he sickened at the name of pleasure, and devoted the whole of his time to study; seldom appearing in the streets, except when his military duties called him abroad, save in the dead of the night, when, secure from interruption, he perambulated the deserted avenues of the city. In one of these nocturnal rambles, a shower of rain obliged him to seek shelter under the porch of a church: the dim light of a lamp, gleaming faintly upon the pavement, caught the gold setting of a locket which, by some accident, was lying on the ground. Wallenstein listlessly picked up the sparkling ornament, and holding it nearer to the light, discovered it to be the miniature portrait of a young and beautiful woman. Though the features were unknown to him, and consequently could not excite any painful feeling, his first impulse was to throw the bauble away; but, ashamed of so childish a sentiment, he placed it in his bosom, and, the night clearing up, went immediately home.

Victor looked very often at the picture; there was a sweet pensive expression in the countenance which sympathised with the present state of his mind; the original was now probably grown old, or was dead, for he had never seen any in the least degree resembling her during his sojourn in the city, and the idea pleased him. He might gaze upon the inanimate object before him without danger: those melting eyes were perchance dim, or closed in the grave—that ruby lip, shrivelled and pale, could no longer deceive the ear of trusting man. This mute companion, so beautiful and so lifeless, unconsciously soothed the tumult in his breast; he wore the picture next to his heart, and in its contemplation forgot the forms of those treacherous beings by whom he had been so deeply injured.

Passing one night through the most ancient and unfrequented part of the city, a street consisting principally of large buildings formerly tenanted by the nobility, but now falling into decay, and converted into magazines and storehouses, he observed that, from the high and narrow windows of the only mansion apparently inhabited by a family of the higher order, streams of brilliant light issued, illuminating the pavement and the opposite wall, and brightly contrasting with the dreariness of the surrounding objects; the sound of music came sweetly upon his ear; he paused to catch the air of a favourite composition. He was standing in the deep shadow of a square tower which flanked the house, and scarcely perceived a low door under a projecting archway beside him; the withdrawing of a rusty bolt aroused his attention; his eyes glanced involuntarily to the place whence the sound proceeded; the door creaked harshly upon its hinges, and a veiled female stole cautiously out. Wallenstein retreated a few paces; the light from the house fell full upon him ; and the lady, for such the richness of her garb indicated her to be, gazed earnestly upon him for the space of a second, then darted forward, and cried, " You look like a man of honour—pity and save me from a fate which I dread worse than death."

Victor wrapped his cloak about the supplicant in an instant, and putting her arm within his, conducted her with speed and safety to his lodgings. A light was burning in the hall, and procuring ready admission by a master-key, he gratified his companion's repeated intreaties for concealment, by ushering her into a private apartment, unseen by any individual. Agitated and weeping, the veil dropped from her hand, and he beheld the original of the miniature !

" Do not think ill of me," she cried, " and do not abuse the trust which unhappy fate has obliged me to repose in a stranger. Afford me shelter for three weeks : I have fled from the persecution of my guardians, who would force me into a marriage with a man that I abhor : their power ends the instant that I become of age ; but, in the interim, should they discover my retreat, the law would compel me to return to them ; and such is the weight and influence of my detested suitor, that I should be conveyed away to one of his castles, and left to the mercy of the most brutal wretch alive. I am rich—alas ! my wealth has been the cause of infinite misery ; but I have not a single friend in the world."

Wallenstein assured her of his protection ; his respectful demeanour disarmed her fears; and she retired to an inner chamber, where a sofa invited her repose, upon his promise that he would keep guard in the street. The night passed quietly away; if any pursuit was made, it did not reach so far, and Victor, at the next meeting with his fair incognita, perceiving that she was unwilling to enter more fully into her history, and flattering himself with the idea that he was perfectly indifferent about it, forbore to ask her any questions. His time was, however, devoted to arrangements for her especial comfort; and it was by no slight exertion of skill and diligence, that he contrived to combine convenience with secresy. He allowed himself only a few hours' rest, in the middle of the day, in an outer apartment, and regularly, throughout every night, paced the streets up and down beneath her window. Their interviews with each other were but few and short, but each seemed equally interested by them. Wallenstein could not long remain proof against the charms of Luitgarde; and the lady, deeply touched by the scrupulous delicacy of her protector's conduct, evinced the most captivating gratitude.

The morning at length came which freed her from the tyranny of her guardians; and Wallenstein, at her request, conducted her to a convent, an asylum which she did not consider to be sufficiently secure before. The whole city now rang with the adventures of the young heiress, who had, almost by a miracle, escaped from the machinations of interested relatives, who had sold her to a man that she hated: they made a futile attempt to reclaim her, but failed. The intemperate effort of the rejected suitor, who even endeavoured to influence the Elector to an act of the grossest injustice, revealed him to a scoffing crowd—it was Prince Albert of Saxe Saalfeldt!

Wallenstein, already many fathoms deep in love, almost adored the lovely creature who had afforded him so signal a triumph over his insulting enemy; and, encouraged by the brightest smiles that ever beamed upon an anxious lover, he threw himself at Luitgarde's feet, and wooed and won the only woman in the world who had ever inspired the libertine destroyer of her sex with a serious attachment.

THE LOVERS OF LYONS.

Their tomb was simple, and without a bust,
And held within their urn, one mind, one heart, one dust.

BYRON.

TRACING the course of the Soane to some distance above Lyons, its banks become most enchantingly romantic : secluded vallies open at intervals on the view, and leave the spectator to penetrate their recesses. These, within themselves, frequently disclose a little world of beauty, where rocks, waterfalls, woods, and streams, are intermingled with scenes of a gentler cast ; where the grape blushes, the grain waves, and the cottage rears its peaceful aspect, with white walls, and flattened roof, half hid by the embowering foliage.

The most distant of these vallies, to which my little excursion extended, surpassed all others in magnificence and loveliness. The uplands, where too steep for culture, were crowned with fine trees ; here thin and scattered, showing between their tall grey stems the most luxuriant herbage, on which sheep were browsing ; there, closely planted and umbrageous, they shed a delicious coolness. Along the bottom, and irregularly indenting the acclivities, were stretched out, in every variety of shape, patches of the richest cultivation ; while a stream of considerable magnitude, pursuing its devious course through these scenes of beauty, by its sound and motion, diffused over the whole an ever-varying charm. Far up the vale, on the summit of a rocky promontory, round whose base swept the stream, in dark eddies, stood the ruins of what had once been a feudal mansion. Though of no great extent, and, as usual, very irregular in its plan, yet the high and pointed gables and turreted embattlements, the massive walls and corner towers, aided by the commanding situation, gave an air of lofty grandeur to the pile. Behind the castle, extending backwards from the stream, was a level tract of considerable extent, gradually subsiding from the slope of the valley. On the nearer portion of this little plain, might still be traced the remains of a garden, its long stone terraces and flights of steps being partly removed, and partly visible among the long withered grass, while all around

Was clothed in living emerald.

In nearly an opposite direction flowed the stream, with the violence of a torrent, being confined in a narrow channel, by lofty and precipitous banks. Across this gulf, considerably above the castle, there appeared to have been a bridge, of which a rude pillar still remained on a mass of rock, rising to some height from the middle of the current. By this means the opposite sides were united, as will appear in the sequel, by a wooden platform.

I had lingered long amid these scenes, and the shades of evening were approaching, before an opportunity occurred of making any inquiry respecting their former history.   Meeting at length with one whose appearance bespoke the easy circumstances of the small *proprietaire*, I began to question him on this subject.   His information, however, extended no farther than that the castle and its domains had originally belonged to the family of De Monthillier, but were now the property of a nobleman who resided in a distant part of the country. To this account a request was added, couched in the politest terms, such as in France frequently surprises the traveller as above the rank of the speaker, "that Monsieur would honour his humble cottage and plain supper, in which case his niece, Augustine, a very good girl, *et qui avoit du sentiment*, would doubtless have much pleasure in relating to Monsieur the history of the last baron." The invitation was too agreeable, and too kindly offered, to be refused.   On arriving at a large and substantial cottage, the old man led the way into a very neat apartment—the floor of shining tiles, scrupulously clean—the walls coarsely but not inelegantly painted in arabesques, to imitate paper-hangings—the bed, the principal ornament, white as snow, and the pillows edged with lace.   Augustine soon made her appearance, with a supper of bread, milk, and grapes, and was, in truth, deserving of the praises bestowed by her uncle.   She was very pretty; and with that frank and lively *naivete* of manner which so peculiarly distinguishes her countrywomen, was united an expression of intelligence and feeling highly interesting.   Our rural repast being soon finished, she gave, with much propriety, a recital which furnished the subject of the following narrative :—

The Baron de Monthillier, the last remaining representative of an ancient and illustrious house, after serving with honour in the armies of his sovereign, had retired to spend, on his paternal domains, the evening of his days, and to superintend the education of his only daughter, the lovely Adelaide. She had been deprived, while yet an infant, of that greatest of all blessings to a youthful female—the care of a tender and accomplished mother. This circumstance had thrown a shade of melancholy over the character and pursuits of the baron, and only in his daughter did he seem to acknowledge the tie which bound him to life. In her he beheld the only solace of his grief, and in watching her improvement he found the most pleasing occupation. Nor was she unworthy of his care. Talents, such as fall to the lot of a few, a disposition the most engaging, and a form the most lovely, marked the rising years of Adelaide.

The baron, his daughter, and her *gouvernante*, an elderly lady of elegant manners and accomplishments, the widow of an officer who had served under her present protector, had for many years composed the only inmates of the castle. At length, in the twelfth year of Adelaide's age, a new event introduced an addition to their domestic circle.

The only sister of the baron had early in life formed an imprudent match,—for such the world presumes to call those connexions which are hallowed by affection, though not recommended by the meaner advantages of wealth or rank. Her husband was by birth a Swiss, in which country he possessed a small property, where his family lived happily, though not splendidly.

His sister had never ceased to be an object of warm affection to the baron ; but the hereditary pride of birth, and dislike of everything like plebian connexion, were among his strongest prejudices. His sister and her husband were equally, but more rationally proud, in disdaining to solicit what they deemed unworthily denied. No intercourse, therefore, had ever been maintained between the separated relatives. In the happiness of domestic duties, in the conversation of the man she loved, and in the education of her only son, this sister, however, never once found cause to regret the sacrifice of useless pomp, for real though humble happiness. But in this life there is no permanent felicity. Before their son, the little Theodore, had attained his seventh year, this kind husband and affectionate parent died.

To his widowed mother, Theodore now remained the only comfort, and to his education she directed all her care. For such a duty, both from ability and affection, no one could be better qualified ; and her son was thus enabled to acquire accomplishments which would have graced any rank. But misfortune seemed to pursue the youthful sufferer. Scarcely had he attained his fourteenth year, when his mother, who had long been in a declining state, breathed her last. Thus, at an age when it is most important to bend the incipient passions to their proper objects, and to accustom them early to control,—at an age where so much may be done towards forming the future character, was he deprived of both his guardians. These were the only reflections which seriously disturbed the death-bed hours of his mother.

She would not leave him, indeed, in want; but who was to watch over his growing years,—to conduct him, with honour and propriety, to manhood? "My brother," she would say, "was ever generous and noble, —he once loved me: and though he, in some measure, disowned our little circle, because I preferred happiness to splendour, he never used me unkindly: surely he will not refuse the dying request of an only and once dear sister. He will not, he cannot deny protection to her orphan child, whom, as the last act of her mortal existence, she recommends to his care." Accordingly she traced, with trembling hand, a few lines to the baron.

"Theodore, my child," said she to her son, a few hours before her death, "when you have laid me by the side of your honoured father, bear this letter to France, to your uncle, the Baron de Monthillier; and, as you have ever been obedient to me, be equally submissive to what your uncle may determine: he is noble and generous, endeavour to merit his approbation, as you would have laboured to deserve my esteem."

The Baron de Monthillier was one evening seated in the apartment where he usually spent that portion of the day with Adelaide and her aged governess, when he was informed that a youthful stranger wished to be introduced. Theodore—for it was he, dressed in the deepest mourning, tall and slender, yet elegant in person, his dark locks curling in profusion round a countenance sweet, indeed, in its expression, but still retaining the strong impress of recent sorrow—then advanced, and presented his mother's letter. A struggle between pride and feeling seemed, for a moment, to agitate the mind of the baron; but the kindlier affections soon obtained the mastery, and he folded his nephew to his bosom.

Theodore had not long been established an inmate in the family of his new protector, when he became a general favourite. In the handsome youth, the baron beheld the image of a long-lost and beloved sister; and in admiring his noble and generous disposition, he almost forgot the imaginary stigma derived from his father's plebeian birth. To the aged friend of his fair cousin, Theodore rendered himself no less agreeable, by the respectful manner in which he was ever solicitous to pay those attentions to which her years and sex entitled her,—attentions not less acceptable, that circumstances no longer enabled her to command them: respect is ever valued in proportion as it is voluntarily shewn, and doubly grateful, in adverse fortune, to those whose undoubted right it once was.

Between the youthful cousins an intimacy still more close was soon established, and cemented by the equality of age—by the agreement of taste—and, in some measure, by the similarity of their pursuits. While Theodore followed his severer studies with ardent application, under a learned monk of a neighbouring monastery, he was not neglectful of more elegant accomplishments, the principles of which he had acquired from the instruction of his excellent mother: these were now prosecuted in company with Adelaide: thus excited, he found himself capable of exertions hitherto unknown, or deemed unattainable.

Gendstaeff

Gaubert, sc

The books which they perused, the languages which they studied, the poets which they read together, possessed charms not to be discovered in their solitary and divided pursuits. Never did music breathe sounds so meltingly sweet—scarcely, indeed, was there harmony to them, when they played not in accompaniment to each other; but, above all, their walks, amid the beautiful and romantic scenery surrounding the chateau, constituted the most delicious moments of existence.

Theodore being fully two years older than his cousin, and the age of the baron, as also of Adelaide's instructress, being such as leads to prefer repose, the youth was taught to consider himself as the protector of the young and lovely being who, on these occasions, clung to him for support. It was, in truth, a sight capable of awakening the deepest interest in their future fate, to behold two beings so young, so beautiful, so amiable, so pure, regarding each other with looks of unutterable affection; each beholding in the other all that was necessary to the happiness of both, yet unconscious whence these feelings sprung, save from the connexion of mere relationship.

Years thus flew rapidly away, unmarked in their flight, and both the cousins were approaching to that maturer age when conscious nature takes the alarm, yet leaves the bosom ignorant of the cause of fear, and dubious of its own feelings. A warmer blush suffused the cheek of Adelaide when pressed by the lips of Theodore, in commendation of some sentiment which she had uttered, or observation she had made; and she dared not as hitherto, yet knew not why, return his caresses. Again, when the hand of his fair cousin pressed affectionately, or by accident, that of the youth, a thrilling sensation, " half ecstacy, half pain," pervaded his whole frame; so sweet, yet so powerful, he hardly knew whether to court or to fear its indulgence : in short both felt, without knowing it, that most delightful of all passions, a first, an early love—a state of felicity in which the human breast can be placed but once, and which is perhaps the purest, the most unalloyed enjoyment which it is, in this life, destined to feel.

But such happiness must be transitory. Theodore was the first to discover the state of his mind, and to perceive his danger : external circumstances, indeed, forced this knowledge upon him, as the flash amidst the darkness of night may disclose to the mariner, the ripple on those breakers of which he slumbered in forgetfulness. War had, some time before, been declared by France against Switzerland, and had continued to be carried on with that violence and cruelty which ever marks a contest between the oppressor and the oppressed, when the latter has once been roused to arms. Theodore loved dearly his country : he therefore began to consider it as dishonourable, thus to forsake her in the hour of danger. What detained him in France ? Alas ! must he confess, even to his own heart, that Adelaide was the cause of his delay. He started at this discovery, as if an abyss had opened at his feet; and the reflections which naturally arose on the occasion, filled his mind with anxiety and regret.

He wished to be gone, yet knew not how to mention the subject to the baron, who intended that his nephew should carry arms in the service of France; although reluctance to a separation had hitherto procrastinated that event. To have now entered into these views, or even to remain inactive, Theodore considered in the highest degree culpable; while his uncle's prejudices in favour of this service were, he knew, very great; and that the execution of the designs which he now meditated, would for ever forfeit his friendship. But were not these views correct? and would not his sainted mother, whose dying words had inculcated obedience to his uncle, have approved them? In the meantime he could only temporise, without resolving on anything but to conceal his intentions both from Adelaide and from her father.

Circumstances, however, produced a crisis sooner than was anticipated. The melancholy and restraint now visible in the deportment of Theodore, could not escape the observation of his cousin, whose penetration was rendered acute by the state of her own heart. One evening, while seated in a small summer-house, which, standing on a romantic steep near the extremity of the grounds surrounding the chateau, usually terminated their walks, the cousins were insensibly betrayed into a conversation, which disclosed to each other their mutual love. Theodore alone concealed his intention of joining the patriot bands of his countrymen.

" But, my dear Adelaide," continued he, " I must leave Monthillier; both prudence and duty dictate my departure. Your father will never consent to our

union, and I cannot think for a moment of betraying
the confidence of my benefactor, or your peace of
mind. I am not worthy of you; I should then be less
so. When you no longer daily see me, your bosom
will recover its wonted serenity."

" Theodore, cruel Theodore!" replied Adelaide;
" do you indeed wish to break my heart? Alas! how
can I, even were it my desire, forget you? Have I
not, for many happy years, been taught to love you
as a brother? Wretched greatness! why should I not
forsake all? Let me go with you to Switzerland; your
parents were happy there—happy in each other; can
we not be so likewise? Ah! what have I said? wretch
that I am, do I forget the duty which a father, a generous and indulgent father, claims?"

Here she burst into tears, and, covering her face
with her hands, wept bitterly; then resuming, in a
calm and subdued tone of voice,

" Theodore, you are right; duty and prudence demand our separation; obtain your uncle's approbation
of your future plans, and the sooner you leave Monthillier the better for us both."

A long silence was only interrupted by the opening
of the door of a small *oratoire* attached to the summer-
house, from which the baron entered. Induced by the
beauty of the evening, he had, contrary to his usual
custom, extended his walk so far; and while engaged
in his devotions, the youthful cousins entered the
summer-house, to whose conversation he had thus
been made an unwilling listener. The trembling lovers
now concluded themselves lost, and, falling on their

knees before the baron, each wished only to implore that his resentment would spare the other. What, then, was their surprise when, looking with the kindest expression on both, the baron addressed them:

" Rise, my children, and in each other receive the reward of your virtue, and of your filial piety. Cherish those sentiments which have hitherto directed your conduct. Theodore, in this trembling hand which I now place in thine, accept the only precious gift which I have to bestow. Rank, birth, and wealth, are to be valued, when, by our station in life, we have to maintain the dignity and the importance of a name, which has descended unsullied to us from illustrious ancestors. Wealth I dispense with. Birth you can claim, at least on one side; rank you may obtain by merit. You are as yet an unknown youth; go and prove to the world that my choice is warranted by nobility of soul; in the ranks of honour acquire renown. You are both young; after a few years' service you may with propriety return to Monthillier, and to Adelaide."

Surprise and astonishment kept Theodore silent; he could only kiss the hand which he still held, and press that of his benefactor to his heart. But short was this gleam of happiness, like the ray, which, for a moment, bursts through the stormy clouds.

" I had written," continued the baron, " without informing you, to the Duke de ——, one of the princes of the blood, my former companion in arms, whose son has been appointed to lead the armies of France against these rebellious mountaineers of the Alps, and you are appointed one of his *aides-de-camp*."

Theodore, summoning all his courage, replied, " I cannot, my lord, accept of this office. I am not insensible of your kindness, nor am I ungrateful ; but I cannot, I dare not, even to gain your approbation, and to deserve Adelaide, fight against my own countrymen."

" How, romantic boy !" exclaimed the baron ; " dost thou then maintain the part of traitors and rebels, because, forsooth, thou deemest barren mountains and rude glens a bond of union. Thou oughtest to reflect that I am interested in thy fortunes, only as the son of my sister, not as the offspring of a Swiss *proprietaire ;* but I give you till to-morrow to fix your determination. Come, Adelaide ;" and before the youth had time to answer, his uncle had departed with the weeping Adelaide.

Theodore, great as was the temptation, required not time to consider whether he ought to accept the conditions on which fortune, and, still more, happiness, were offered. After writing to his uncle, and putting himself in possession of the details respecting his little property, the same night beheld him on his way to his oppressed country.

Months rolled on without soothing the sorrows of Adelaide.

> Oh grief, beyond all other griefs, when fate
> First leaves the young heart lone and desolate,
> In the wide world, without the only tie
> For which it loved to live or feared to die ;—
> Lorn as the hung-up lute, that ne'er hath spoken
> Since the sad day its master-chord was broken !

Nor was this sorrow lessened by the addresses of another suitor, in the son of the Count de ———, whose domains lay contiguous to the lands of Monthillier. Her father, without pressing the match, gave her to understand, that a union in every respect so suitable would be agreeable to him. Externally, this young nobleman appeared to possess all the qualities which could render a woman happy; but this appearance of virtue was merely superficial: he was selfish and avaricious, though addicted to pleasure. He beheld, indeed, with admiration, the beauty of Adelaide; but her fortune was to him the greatest charm. Adelaide, in part penetrated his character, but to the baron he appeared unexceptionable, and his daughter only beheld in delay a dubious and temporary relief.

In the meantime the power of the invaders proved irresistible in Switzerland; and Theodore, after exertions which had greatly signalized him, saw his unhappy country totally subdued. A wanderer and an exile, he was indebted for his personal safety, as well as present liberty, to the gratitude of the French commander—the very nobleman under whom he had been appointed to serve, whose life he had saved at the imminent risk of his own. The French general, attended only by a few officers and a small escort, had advanced to some distance from his camp, for the purpose of observing the enemy's position. This being observed by Theodore, who held a conspicuous station among the patriot leaders, he quickly assembled an active and intrepid party, with which, taking a circuitous route, he succeeded, after a sharp conflict, in carrying off the general and several of his officers prisoners. A short time previous to this event, some Swiss officers, either were, or were reported to have been murdered in cold blood by their invaders, and it was now determined to retaliate this barbarity. Theodore stood bravely forward in defence of his unfortunate captives, and declared, that only with life would he cease to defend those who had submitted on his pledge of security. A bad action frequently requires only one vigorous opponent to be defeated. So it was on the present occasion, and the prisoners were allowed to be ransomed.

Abandoning his enslaved country, where he now possessed nothing, and actuated by that restless anxiety which, in misery, urges us to revisit the scenes of former happiness, Theodore, almost without intending it, found himself in Lyons. So near, ought he not to trace once more the walks and shades of Monthillier— might he not be allowed to gaze, for the last time, on Adelaide, while he himself remained unseen? Such were his reflections; and the rays of the evening sun were falling brightly on the little summer-house, the scene of his last delusive interview, as he gazed upon it from the opposite bank of the stream. To this, except by going close to the castle, there was only one passage, over a narrow bridge of wood, which here spanned the gulf, at a great height above the torrent. By the shade of impending rocks and surrounding woods, this place was gloomy even at noon-day; but when the shadows of evening had closed around, the rustic bridge was involved in almost total darkness. By this path, which long habit had rendered at all hours familiar to him,

Theodore now entered those precincts so often trodden with pleasure, and soon found himself at the door of the elegant little building, which still continued to be the favourite retreat of Adelaide.

No one was there, but a book lay open on the table. This Theodore recognised as an Italian classic which he had frequently read with Adelaide. He pressed the unconscious volume to his lips and to his bosom, and ere he was aware, Adelaide herself entered. In mute astonishment, she suffered him to take her hand, and lead her to a seat. She could not speak—tears at length came to her relief. Of many things did the lovers discourse, without coming to any resolution, save to meet again.

The interview had not passed without observation. The new lover of Adelaide had gained over to his purposes a confidential domestic in the family of the baron. This person, agreeably to his instructions, watching every movement of Adelaide, had discovered the meeting of the cousins, and had also traced Theodore to a neighbouring cottage, where he intended to remain concealed for a few days, as he hoped soon to receive letters which might facilitate a reconciliation with his uncle.

Informed of Theodore's return, and of the meeting with Adelaide, the young count set no bounds to his desire of vengeance, and resolved, at all hazards, to remove his rival. Yet he was at a loss how to proceed. Should he inform the baron, the young lady would doubtless be confined; but this would rather increase her dislike to the author of such an outrage. Again, should he challenge his opponent,—for the count was

deficient neither in skill, nor in that vilest of all qualities which has obtained, through prejudice, the name of
virtue—mere courage; still the consequences, as regarded the aversion of Adelaide, would be the same,
while the issue might prove fatal to the contriver.   No
other method then remained, but to take off Theodore
by some secret means.

   In order to mature his purposes, he determined himself to be a witness of the lovers' second interview.
The sun was just sinking beneath the western horizon,
when he beheld Theodore hasten along the narrow and
half overgrown pathway across the deep ravine, and
enter the summer-house: a few minutes after, Adelaide
appeared in an opposite direction, proceeding from the
castle.   Still lurking amid the underwood, the count
continued to expect the termination of their conference.   At length the youthful pair were seen advancing
from the pavilion; they approached so close to the
spot where the count lay concealed, for he had come
nearer on purpose to overhear their discourse, that he
caught the softness of Adelaide's voice, in a subdued
manner, urging her lover to suffer in patience, adding,
in such accents as a ministering angel would employ
to soothe the troubled soul—" My father is not inexorable, and the interest of those friends whom you
mention I know to be great; at all events, the happiness of another interview awaits us—we meet again
to-morrow."   The sounds were now indistinct, but the
count had obtained the desired information: he continued to watch their motions.   Theodore accompanied
Adelaide till nearly within view of the castle; then

bidding a hasty adieu, he struck into a more secluded path, which conducted to the bridge across the ravine, and thence to the cottage where he had fixed his temporary abode.

The count now exulted in the certain prospect of accomplishing his designs. The lovers were to meet on the succeeding eve. Theodore had but one way to pass; total darkness would then involve the bed of the torrent, and the bridge, by which alone it could be crossed : nothing could be more easy than, before the youth's return, to remove a few of the transverse planks composing the platform, and the hapless passenger would drop—unseen, unheard—into the gulf beneath: the planks being restored, the secret of his fate would remain concealed from all.

The evening sun shone brightly, with " farewell sweet," as the count, too faithful to his purpose, repaired to his lurking place. Not long after, Theodore was seen advancing with ardent and impatient steps, possibly unconscious of everything but the delight of meeting Adelaide ; nor were his anticipations disappointed ; scarcely had he attained the walk leading to the pavilion when she appeared, and both entered. The count eyed the place with a look of savage joy, as the couching tiger glares upon the prey now within its spring : as darkness advanced he proceeded to remove the boards, which he had previously loosened, from the fatal bridge, leaving a yawning chasm in the narrow footway over the deepest part of the abyss.

In the meantime the lovers were delighting themselves with prospects of future happiness, which now, indeed, seemed no longer delusive. Theodore had that day received letters from the Prince de ———, the French commander, whose life he saved in Switzerland; this generous friend had not forgotten the obligation, and had so represented the matter to his sovereign, that Theodore's little estate was not only restored, but the King had invested him with the honour of knighthood, and, farther, offered him an honourable rank in his army. Theodore could now have no objection to accept of these favours, and the only remaining difficulty was, to obtain the consent and forgiveness of his uncle : of this Adelaide did not despair, as she believed her father had also received letters to the same import, for he had that day, for the first time since his departure, mentioned the name of Theodore, saying " he was happy to hear, for his own sake, that the youth had not acted so dishonourably as he had been led to believe." It was therefore determined that Theodore should immediately request an interview with the baron, and that Adelaide should expect the result in the pavilion.

The interview between the relatives was cordial; many things, however, were to be explained, and considerable space elapsed in the conference between Theodore and his uncle.

Adelaide, in the interval, could not feel composed, while her happiness was thus at stake, and her future life trembling on the point of decision. Tired of repose, she began to pace the small apartment included within the circuit of the pavilion. Motion of body, she thought, gave her mind ease, and she continued her walk in the open air. In this state of anxiety, every place was alike indifferent, and every spot equally well known. Without surprise, then, for it was at no great distance from the summer-house, she found her steps had been unconsciously directed to the rustic bridge. " The fresh air will cool my feverish brow," thought she, and advanced. Her light foot was heard for a moment on the platform —it ceased—a faint and convulsive shriek—a heavy plunge, sounding for an instant above the roar of the torrent, told the fate of the young and lovely victim.

The baron and Theodore were now reconciled. Everything had been explained to the old man's satisfaction.

" But where is Adelaide?" said he, with impatient satisfaction in his accents; " why does not she participate in the happiness of this moment?"

"I go to call her," said Theodore; " my cousin waits in the pavilion."

They were at this time in a recess formed by a corner turret, built on the very verge of the rock on which the castle stood, and where two windows overlooked the stream. At this moment something white floating on its surface, caught the eye of Theodore. A sad presentiment seized his mind—he rushed from the apartment, descended the rocks with fearful rapidity, and clasped the body of the lifeless Adelaide.

What words can describe the frantic grief of the hapless lover, or the speechless sorrow of the aged parent! Happily the sufferings of the latter were of short duration. He died before the morning rays dawned on his wretchedness.

Three days did Theodore watch the beloved remains in silent and solitary woe. On the fourth, the funeral obsequies were solemnized. When the last of the hallowed mould had been placed upon their graves, and when the crowd of mourners was now lessening, " Hast thou at last broken ?" exclaimed the youth, speaking, for the first time, and laying his hand on his heart, as he sunk upon the ground. Then in scarcely audible accents, " Lay me," said he, " by Adelaide !" and expired.

The wretch who had occasioned all these calamities had alone been privy to his own machinations. But the confession of the baron's domestic whom he had seduced to act as a spy, was sufficient to implicate him in suspicion. The count was therefore arrested, and agonised by remorse, at last voluntarily confessed his guilt. Between his sentence and execution, however, reason deserted her throne ; a raving maniac, he survived many years a fearful example of the effects of crime, and enduring a punishment more terrible than death itself.

THE MERCHANT OF BREMEN.

Sir Ryence of North Gales greeteth well thee,
And bids thee thy beard anon to him send,
Or else from thy jaws he will it off rend.
Percy's Reliques of Ancient English Poetry.

THERE formerly lived at Bremen, a wealthy merchant named Melchoir, of whom it was remarked, that he invariably stroked his chin with complacency, whenever the subject of the sermon was the rich man in the Gospel; who, by the bye, in comparison with him, was only a petty retail dealer. This said Melchoir possessed such great riches, that he caused the floor of his dining-room to be paved with crown pieces, which ridiculous luxury gave great offence to his fellow-citizens and relations. They attributed it to vanity and ostentation, but did not guess its true motive; however, it perfectly answered the end Melchoir designed by it; for by their constantly expressing their disapprobation of this ostentatious species of vanity, they spread abroad the report of their neighbour's immense riches, and thereby augmented his credit in a most astonishing manner.

At length Melchoir died suddenly, while at a corporation dinner, and consequently had not time to make a disposition of his property by will; so that his only son Francis, who was just of age, came in possession of the whole. This young man was particularly favoured

P

by fortune, both with respect to his personal advantages and his goodness of heart; but this immense inheritance caused his ruin.   He had no sooner got into the possession of so considerable a fortune, than he squandered it, as if it had been a burthen to him; ran into every possible extravagance, and neglected his concerns. Two or three years passed over without his perceiving that, owing to his dissipations, his funds were considerably diminished; but at length his coffers were emptied: and one day, when Francis had drawn a draft to a very considerable amount on his banker, who had no funds to meet it, it was returned to him protested.   This disappointment greatly vexed our prodigal, but only as it caused a temporary check to his wishes; for he did not even then give himself the trouble to enquire into the reason of it.   After swearing and blustering for some time, he gave his steward a positive but laconic order to *get money*.

All the brokers, bankers, money-changers, and usurers, were put in requisition, and the empty coffers were soon filled; for the dining-room floor was in the eyes of the lenders a sufficient security.

This palliative had its effect for a time; but all at once a report was spread abroad in the city that the celebrated silver floor had been taken up; the consequence of which was, that the lenders insisted on examining into and proving the fact, and then became urgent for payment: but as Francis had not the means to meet their demands, they seized on all his goods and chattels; everything was sold by auction, and he had nothing left excepting a few jewels, which had formed part of his heritage, and which might for a short time keep him from starving.

He now took up his abode in a small street in one of the most remote quarters of the city, where he lived on his straitened means. He, however, accommodated himself to his situation; but the only resource he found against the *ennui* which overpowered him, was to play on the lute; and when fatigued by this exercise, he used to stand at his window and make observations on the weather; and his intelligent mind was not long in discovering an object which soon entirely engrossed his thoughts.

Opposite his window their lived a respectable woman, who was at her spinning wheel from morning till night, and by her industry earned a subsistence for herself and her daughter. Meta was a young girl of great beauty and attraction: she had known happier times; for her father had been the proprietor of a vessel freighted by himself, in which he annually made trading voyages to Antwerp; but he, as well as his ship and all its cargo, was lost in a violent storm. His widow sustained this double loss with resignation and firmness, and resolved to support herself and her daughter by her own industry. She made over the house and furniture to the creditors of her husband, and took up her abode in the little bye street in which Francis lodged, where by her assiduity she acquired a subsistence without laying herself under an obligation to any one. She brought up her daughter to spinning and other work, and lived with so much economy, that by her savings she was enabled to set up a little trade in linen.

Mother Bridget (which was the appellation given to our widow) did not, however, calculate on terminating her existence in this penurious situation; and the hope of better prospects sustained her courage. The beauty and excellent qualities of her daughter, whom she brought up with every possible care and attention, led her to think that some advantageous offer would one day present itself. Meta lived tranquilly and lonely with her mother, was never seen in any of the public walks, and indeed never went out but to mass once a day.

One day, while Francis was making his meteorological observations at the window, he saw the beautiful Meta, who, under her mother's watchful eye, was returning from church. The heart of Francis was as yet quite free; for the boisterous pleasures of his past life did not leave him leisure for a true affection; but at this time, when all his senses were calm, the appearance of one of the most enchanting female forms he had ever seen, ravished him, and he henceforth thought solely of the adorable object which his eyes had thus discovered. He questioned his landlord respecting the two females who lived in the opposite house, and from him learned the particulars we have just related.

He now regretted his want of economy, since his present miserable state prevented him from making an offer to the charming Meta. He was, however, constantly at the window, in hopes of seeing her; and in that consisted his greatest delight. The mother very soon discovered the frequent appearance of her new neighbour at his window, and attributed it to its right cause. In consequence, she rigorously enjoined her daughter not to shew herself at the windows, which were now kept constantly shut.

Francis was not much versed in the arts of finesse, but love awakened all the energies of his soul. He soon discovered that if he appeared much at the window, his views would be suspected; and he resolved, therefore, studiously to refrain from coming near it. He determined, however, to continue his observation of what occurred in the opposite dwelling, without being perceived. He accordingly purchased a large mirror, and fixed it in his chamber in such a position that it distinctly presented to his view what passed in the abode of his opposite neighbour.

Francis not being seen at the window, the old lady relaxed in her rigour, and Meta's windows were once more opened. Love, more than ever, reigned triumphant in the bosom of Francis; but how was he to make known his attachment to its object? He could neither speak nor write to her. Love, however, soon suggested a mode of communication which succeeded. Our prodigal took his lute, and drew from it tones the best adapted to express the subject of his passion; and by perseverance, in less than a month he made a wonderful progress. He soon had the gratification of seeing the fair hand of Meta open the little casement, when he began to tune the instrument. When she made her appearance, he testified his joy by an air lively and gay; but if she did not shew herself, the melancholy softness of his tones discovered the disappointment he experienced.

In the course of a short time he created a great interest in the bosom of his fair neighbour, and soon had reason to be convinced that Meta shared a mutual attachment. She now endeavoured to justify him, when her mother with acrimony spoke of his prodigality and past misconduct, by attributing his ruin to the effect of bad example. But in doing so, she cautiously avoided exciting the suspicions of the old lady; and seemed less anxious to excuse him, than to take a part in the conversation which was going on.

Various untoward circumstances had, by this time, rendered the situation of Francis more and more difficult to be supported: his funds had now nearly failed him, and an offer of marriage from a wealthy brewer, who was called in the neighbourhood the "King of Hops," but which Meta, much to her mother's disappointment, refused, excited still more the apprehension of poor Francis, lest some more fortunate suitor might yet be received, and blast his hopes for ever.

When he received the information that this opulent lover had been rejected for his sake, with what bitterness did he lament his past follies.

"Generous girl," said he, "you sacrifice yourself for a miserable creature, who has nothing but a heart fondly attached to you, and which is riven with despair that its possessor cannot offer you the happiness you so truly merit."

The King of Hops soon found another female, who listened more kindly to his vows, and whom he wedded with great splendour.

Love, however, did not leave his work incomplete; for its influence created in the mind of Francis a desire of exerting his faculties, and actively employing himself, in order, if possible, to emerge from the state of nothingness into which he was at present plunged; and it inspired him also with courage to prosecute his good intentions. Among various projects which he formed, the most rational appeared that of overlooking his father's books, taking an account of the claimable debts, and from that source to get all he possibly could. The produce of this procedure would, he thought, furnish him with the means of beginning in some small way of business, and his imagination led him to extend this to the most remote corners of the earth. In order to equip himself for the prosecution of his plans, he sold all the remainder of his father's effects, and with the money purchased a horse to commence his travels.

The idea of a separation from Meta was almost more than he could endure. " What will she think," said he, " of this sudden disappearance, when she no longer meets me in her way to church? Will she not think me perfidious, and banish me from her heart?" Such ideas as these caused him infinite pain, and for a long while he could not devise any means of acquainting Meta with his plans; but at length the fertile genius of love furnished him with the following idea :—Francis went to the curate of the church which his mistress daily frequented, and requested him, before the sermon, and during mass, to put up prayers for *a happy issue to the affairs of a young traveller;* and these prayers were to be continued till the moment of his return, when they were to be changed into those of thanks.

Every thing being arranged for his departure, he mounted his steed, and passed close under Meta's window : he saluted her with a very significant air, and with much less caution than heretofore. The young girl blushed deeply, and mother Bridget took this opportunity of loudly expressing her dislike to this bold adventurer, whose impertinence and foppery induced him to form designs on her daughter.

From this period the eyes of Meta in vain searched for Francis. She constantly heard the prayer which was put up for him; but was so entirely absorbed by grief at no longer perceiving the object of her affection, that she paid no attention to the words of the priest. In no way could she account for his disappearing. Some months afterwards, her grief being somewhat ameliorated, and her mind more tranquillized, when she was one day thinking of the last time she had seen Francis, the prayer arrested her attention; she reflected for an instant, and quickly divined for whom it was said; she naturally joined in it with great fervour, and strongly recommended the young traveller to the protection of her guardian angel.

Meanwhile Francis continued his journey, and had travelled the whole of a very sultry day, over one of the desert cantons of Westphalia, without meeting with a single house; as night approached a violent storm came on, the rain fell in torrents, and poor Francis was soaked to the very skin. In this miserable situation he anxiously looked around, and fortunately discovered in the distance a light, towards which he directed his horse's steps; but, as he drew near, he beheld a miserable cottage, which did not promise him much succour, for it more resembled a stable than the habitation of a human being. The unfeeling wretch who inhabited it refused him fire or water, as if he had been a banished man—he was just about to extend himself on the straw in the midst of the cattle, and his indolence prevented his lighting a fire for the stranger. Francis vainly endeavoured to move the peasant to pity; the latter was inexorable, and blew out his candle with the greatest *nonchalance* possible, without bestowing a thought on Francis. However, as the traveller hindered him from sleeping, by his incessant lamentations and prayers, he was anxious to get rid of him.

" Friend," said he to him, " if you wish to be accommodated, I promise you it will not be here; but ride through the little wood to your left hand, and you will find the castle belonging to the chevalier Eberhard Bronkhorst, who is very hospitable to travellers; but he has a singular mania, which is, to flagellate all whom he entertains, therefore decide accordingly."

Francis, after considering for some minutes, resolved on hazarding the adventure. " In good faith," said he, " there is no great difference between having one's back broken by the miserable accommodation of a peasant, or by the chevalier Bronkhorst; friction dis-

perses fever, possibly its effects may prove beneficial
to me, if I am compelled to keep on my wet garments.''

Accordingly he put spurs to his horse, and very
shortly found himself before a gothic castle, at the
iron gate of which he loudly knocked, and was answered from within by—'' *Who's there*?'' But ere he
was allowed time to reply, the gate was opened. However, in the first court he was compelled to wait with
patience, till they could learn whether it was the lord
of the castle's pleasure to flagellate a traveller, or send
him out to pass the night under the canopy of heaven.

. This lord of the castle had, from his earliest infancy,
served in the imperial army, under the command of
George of Frunsberg, and had himself led a company
of infantry against the Venetians : at length, however,
fatigued with warfare, he had retired to his own territory, where, in order to expiate the crimes he had
committed during the several campaigns he had been in,
he did all the good and charitable acts in his power ;
but his manner still preserved all the roughness of his
former profession.   The newly arrived guest, although
disposed to submit to the usages of the house, for the
sake of the good fare, could not help feeling a certain
trembling of fear as he heard the bolts grating, ere the
doors were opened to him ; and which, by their groan-
ing noise, seemed to presage the catastrophe which
awaited him : a cold perspiration came over him as he
passed the last door ; but finding that he received the
utmost attention, his fears a little abated. . The servants assisted him in getting off his horse, and unfas-

tened his cloak-bag; some of them led his horse to
the stable, whilst others preceding him with flambeaux,
conducted him to their master, who awaited his arrival
in a room magnificently lighted up.

. Poor Francis was seized with an universal tremor,
when he beheld the martial air and athletic form of the
lord of the castle, who came up to him and shook him
by the hand with so much force as nearly to make him
cry out, and, in a thundering voice enough to stun
him, told him " he was welcome." Francis trembled
like an aspen-leaf in every part of his body.

" What ails you, my young comrade ?" cried the
chevalier Bronkhorst, " what makes you thus tremble,
and render you as pale as if death had actually seized
you by the throat ?"

Francis recovered himself; and knowing that his
shoulders would pay the reckoning, his fears gave
place to a species of audacity.

. " My lord," answered he, with confidence, " you
see that I am so soaked with rain that one might suppose I had swam through the Wezer ; order me, therefore, some dry clothes instead of those I have on, and
let us then drink a cup of hot wine, that I may, if
possible, prevent the fever which otherwise may probably seize me : it will comfort my heart."

" Admirable !" replied the chevalier ; " ask for
whatever you want, and consider yourself here as at
home."

Accordingly, Francis gave his orders like a baron of
high degree : he sent away the wet clothes, made
choice of others, and, in fine, made himself quite at

his ease. The chevalier, so far from expressing any dissatisfaction at his free and easy manners, commanded his people to execute whatever he ordered with promptitude, and condemned some of them as blockheads, who did not appear to know how to wait on a stranger. As soon as the table was spread, the chevalier seated himself at it with his guest, and they drank a cup of hot wine together.

" Do you wish for any thing to eat?" demanded the lord.

Francis desired he would order up what his house afforded, that he might see whether his kitchen was good.

No sooner had he said this than the steward made his appearance, and soon furnished up a most delicious repast. Francis did not wait for his being requested to partake of it; but after having made a hearty meal, he said to the lord of the castle, " your kitchen is by no means despicable; if your cellar is correspondent, I cannot but say you treat your guest nobly."

The chevalier made a sign to his butler, who brought up some inferior wine, and filled a large glass of it to his master, who drank to his guest. Francis instantly returned the compliment.

" Well, young man, what say you to my wine?" asked the chevalier.

" 'Faith," replied Francis, " I say it is bad, if it is the best you have in your cellar; but if you have none worse, I do not condemn it."

" You are a connoisseur;" answered the chevalier. " Butler, bring us a flask of older wine."

His orders being instantly attended to, Francis tasted it. "This is indeed some good old wine, and we will stick to it if you please."

The servants brought in a great pitcher of it, and the chevalier, being in high good-humour, drank freely with his guest; and then launched out into a long history of his several feats of prowess in the war against the Venetians. He became so overheated by the recital, that in his enthusiasm he overturned the bottles and glasses, and flourishing his knife as if it were a sword, passed it so near the nose and ears of Francis, that he dreaded he should lose them in the action.

Though the night wore away, the chevalier did not manifest any desire to sleep; for he was quite in his element, whenever he got on the topic of the Venetian war. Each succeeding glass added to the heat of his imagination as he proceeded in his narration, till at length Francis began to apprehend that it was the prologue to the tragedy in which he was to play the principal part; and feeling anxious to learn whether he was to pass the night in the castle, or to be turned out, he asked for a last glass of wine to enable him to sleep well. He feared that they would commence by filling him with wine, and that if he did not consent to continue drinking, a pretext would be laid hold of for driving him out of the castle with the usual chastisement.

However, contrary to his expectation, the lord of the castle broke the thread of his narration, and said to him: "Good friend, everything in its place: to-morrow we will resume our discourse."

"Excuse me, sir knight," replied Francis: "to-morrow, before sun-rise, I shall be on my road. The distance from hence to Brabant is very considerable, and I cannot tarry here longer, therefore permit me to take leave of you now, that I may not disturb you in the morning."

" Just as you please about that ; but you will not leave the castle before I am up : we will breakfast together, and I shall accompany you to the outer gate, and take leave of you according to my usual custom."

Francis needed no comment to render these words intelligible. Most willingly would he have dispensed with the chevalier's company to the gate ; but the latter did not appear at all inclined to deviate from his established usage. He ordered his servant to assist the stranger in undressing, and to take care of him till he was in bed.

Francis found his bed an excellent one ; and ere he went to sleep, he owned that so handsome a reception could not be dearly bought at the expence of a *trifling* beating. The most delightful dreams (in which Meta bore the sway) occupied him the whole night; and he would have gone on (thus dreaming) till mid-day, if the sonorous voice of the chevalier, and the clanking of his spurs, had not disturbed him.

It needed all Francis's efforts to quit this delightful bed, in which he was so comfortable, and where he knew himself to be in safety : he turned from side to side ; but the chevalier's tremendous voice was like a death-stroke to him, and at length he resolved to get up. Several servants assisted him in dressing, and the chevalier waited for him at a small but well-served table; but Francis, knowing the moment of trial was at hand, had no great inclination to feast. The chevalier tried to persuade him to eat, telling him it was the best thing to keep out the fog and damp air of the morning.

"Sir knight," replied Francis, "my stomach is still loaded from your excellent supper of last evening; but my pockets are empty, and I should much like to fill them, in order to provide against future wants."

The chevalier evinced his pleasure at his frankness, by filling his pockets with as much as they could contain. As soon as they brought him his horse, which he discovered had been well groomed and fed, he drank the last glass of wine to say adieu, expecting that, at that signal, the chevalier would take him by the collar and make him pay his welcome; but, to his no small surprise, the chevalier contented himself with heartily shaking him by the hand as on his arrival, and as soon as the gate was opened, Francis rode off safe and sound.

In no way could our traveller account for his host permitting him thus to depart without paying the usual score; at length he began to imagine that the peasant had simply told him the story to frighten him, and feeling a curiosity to learn whether or not it had any foundation in fact, he rode back to the castle. The chevalier had not yet quitted the gate, and was conversing with his servants on the pace of Francis's horse, who appeared to trot very roughly; and seeing the traveller return, he supposed that he had forgotten

something, and by his looks seemed to accuse his servants of negligence.

"What do you want, young man?" demanded he:
"Why do you, who were so much pressed for time,
return?"

"Allow me, most noble sir," replied Francis, "to
ask you one question, for there are reports abroad
which tend to villify you: it is said that, after having
hospitably received and entertained strangers, you
make them, at their departure, feel the weight of your
arm; and although I gave credence to this rumour, I
have omitted nothing which might have entitled me to
this mark of your favour; but, strange to say, you
have permitted me to depart in peace, without even the
slightest mark of your strength. You see my surprise,
therefore do pray inform me whether there is any foundation for the report, or whether I shall chastise the
impudent story-teller who related the false tale to me."

"Young man," replied Bronkhorst, "you have heard
nothing but the truth; but it needs some explanations.
I open my door hospitably to every stranger, and in
christian charity I give them a place at my table; but
I am a man who hates form or disguise: I say all I
think, and only wish in return that my guests openly
and undisguisedly ask for all they want. There are unfortunately, however, a tribe of people who fatigue
by their mean complaisance and ceremony, who wear
me out by their dissimulation, and stun me by pro-
popositions devoid of sense, or who do not conduct
themselves with decency during the repast. Gracious

heavens! I lose all patience when they carry their fooleries to such excess, and I exert my right as master of the castle, by taking hold of their collars, and giving them a tolerably severe chastisement ere I turn them out of my gates : but a man of your sort, my young friend, will ever be welcome under my roof; for you boldly and openly ask for what you require, and say what you think, and such are the persons I admire: if in your way back you pass through this canton, promise me you will pay me another visit—Good bye. Let me caution you never to place implicit confidence in anything you hear; believe only that there may be a single grain of truth in the whole story; be always frank, and you will succeed through life. Heaven's blessings attend you."

Francis continued his journey towards Anvers most gaily, wishing, as he went, that he might everywhere meet with as good a reception as at the chevalier Bronkhorst's.

Nothing remarkable occurred during the rest of his journey, and he entered the city full of the most sanguine hopes and expectations. In every street his fancied riches stared him in the face. " It appears to me," said he, " that some of my father's debtors must have succeeded in business, and that they will only require my presence, to repay their debts with honour."

After having rested from the fatigue of his journey, he made himself acquainted with every particular relative to the debtors, and learnt that the greater part had become rich, and were doing extremely well. This

Q

intelligence re-animated his hopes; he arranged his
papers, and payed a visit to each of the persons who
owed him anything.   But his success was by no means
equal to what he had expected; some of the debtors
pretended that they had paid every thing, others that
they had never heard mention of Melchoir of Bremen,
and the rest produced accounts precisely contradictory
to those he had, and which tended to prove they were
creditors instead of debtors: in fine, ere three days
had elapsed, Francis found himself in the debtor's
prison, from whence he stood no chance of being released till he had paid the uttermost farthing of his
father's debts.

How pitiable was this poor young man's condition!
Even the horrors of the prison were augmented by the
remembrance of Meta; nay, to such a pitch of desperation was he carried, that he resolved to starve himself: fortunately, however, at twenty-seven years of
age, such determinations are more easily formed than
practised.

The intention of those who put him into confine-
ment was not merely with a view of exacting payment
of his pretended debts, but to avoid paying him his
due; so whether the prayers put up for poor Francis
at Bremen were effectual, or that the pretended creditors were not disposed to maintain him during his
life, I know not; but, after a detention of three
months, they liberated Francis from prison, with a
particular injunction to quit the territories of Anvers
within four-and-twenty hours, and never to set his foot
within that city again: they gave him, at the same

time, five florins to defray his expences on the road. As one may well imagine, his horse and baggage had been sold to defray the costs incident to the proceedings.

With a heart overloaded with grief he quitted Anvers, in a very different frame of mind to what he experienced at entering it. Discouraged and irresolute, he mechanically followed the road which chance directed; he paid no attention to the various travellers, or indeed to any object on the road, till hunger or thirst caused him to lift his eyes to discover a steeple, or some other token announcing the habitation of human beings. In this state of mind did he continue journeying on for several days incessantly; nevertheless, a secret instinct impelled him to take the road leading to his own country.

All on a sudden he roused, as if from a profound sleep, and recollected the place in which he was: he stopped an instant to consider whether he should continue the road he was then in, or return—" For," said he, " what a shame to return to my native city a beggar!" How could he thus return to that city in which he formerly felt equal to the richest of its inhabitants? How could he as a beggar present himself before Meta, without causing her to blush for the choice she had made? He did not allow time for his imagination to complete this miserable picture, for he instantly turned back, as if already he had found himself before the gates of Bremen, followed by the shouts of the children. His mind was soon made up as to what he should do: he resolved to go to one of the ports of the Low Countries, there to engage himself as a sailor on board a Spanish vessel, to go to the newly-discovered world; and not to return to his native country till he had amassed as much wealth as he had formerly so thoughtlessly squandered. In the whole of this project, Meta was only thought of at an immeasurable distance; but Francis contented himself with connecting her in idea with his future plans, and walked, or rather strode along, as if by hurrying his pace he should sooner gain possession of her.

Having thus attained the frontiers of the Low Countries, he arrived at the sunset in a village situated near Rheinburg, but since entirely destroyed in the thirty years' war. A caravan of carriers from Liege filled the inn so entirely, that the landlord told Francis he could not give him a lodging; adding, that at the adjoining village he would find accommodations. Possibly he was actuated to this refusal by Francis's appearance, who certainly, in point of garb, might well be mistaken for a vagabond.

The landlord took him for a spy to a band of thieves, sent probably to rob the carriers; so that poor Francis, spite of his extreme lassitude, was compelled, with his wallet at his back, to proceed on his road; and having, at his departure, muttered through his teeth some bitter maledictions against the cruel and unfeeling landlord, the latter appeared touched with compassion for the poor stranger, and from the door of the inn called after him : " Young man—a word with you ! If you resolve on passing the night here, I will procure you a lodging in that castle you now see on the hill; there you will have rooms in abundance, provided you are not afraid of being alone, for it is uninhabited. See, here are the keys belonging to it."

Francis joyfully accepted the landlord's proposition, and thanked him for it as if it had been an act of great charity.

" It is to me a matter of little moment where I pass the night, provided I am at my ease, and have something to eat." But the landlord was an ill-tempered fellow, and wishing to revenge the invectives Francis had poured forth against him, he sent him to the castle in order that he might be tormented by the spirits which were said to frequent it.

This castle was situated on a steep rock, and was only separated from the village by the high road and a little rivulet. Its delightful prospects caused it to be kept in good repair, and to be well furnished, as its owner made use of it as a hunting seat; quitting it, however, every night, in order to avoid the apparitions and ghosts which haunted it.

When it was quite dark, Francis, with a lantern in his hand, proceeded towards the castle. The landlord accompanied him, and carried a little basket of provisions, to which he had added a bottle of wine, (which he said would stand the test,) as well as two candles and two wax tapers for the night. Francis, not thinking he should require so many things, and being apprehensive he should have to pay for them, asked why they were all brought.

" The light from my lantern," said he, " will suffice me till the time of my getting into bed ; and ere I shall get out of it the sun will have risen, for I am quite worn out with fatigue."

" I will not endeavour to conceal from you," replied the landlord, " that according to the current reports, this castle is haunted by evil spirits ; but do not let that frighten you—you see I live sufficiently near that, in case anything extraordinary should happen to you, I can hear you call, and shall be in readiness with my people to render you any assistance; at my house there is somebody stirring all night, and there is also some one constantly on the watch. I have lived on this spot for thirty years, and cannot say that I have ever seen anything to alarm me; indeed, I believe that you may with safety attribute any noises you hear during the night in this castle, to cats and weasels, with which the granaries are overrun. I have only provided you with the means of keeping up a light in case of need, for, at best, night is but a gloomy season; and, in addition, these candles are consecrated, and their light will undoubtedly keep off any evil spirits, should there be such in the castle."

The landlord spoke only the truth, when he said he had not seen any ghosts in the castle, for he never had the courage to set his foot within its doors after dark ; and though he now spoke so courageously, the rogue would not have ventured on any account to enter. After having opened the door, he gave the basket to Francis, pointed out the way he was to turn, and wished him good night ; while the latter, fully satisfied that the story of the ghosts must be fabulous, gaily entered. He recollected all that had been told him to the prejudice of the chevalier Bronkhorst, but unfortunately forgot what that brave Castellan had recommended to him at parting, " always to believe there was some truth in what he might hear."

Conformably to the landlord's instructions, he went up stairs, and came to a door, which the key in his possession soon unlocked : it opened into a long dark gallery, where his very steps re-echoed : this gallery led to a large hall, from which issued a suite of apartments furnished in a costly manner : he surveyed them all, and made choice of one in which to pass the night that appeared rather more lively than the rest; the windows looked to the high road, and everything that passed in front of the inn could be distinctly heard. He lighted two candles, spread the cloth, ate very heartily, and felt completely at his ease, so long as he was thus employed, for while eating no thought or apprehension of spirits molested him ; but he no sooner arose from table, than he began to feel a sensation strongly resembling fear.

In order to render himself secure, he locked the door, drew the bolts, and then looked out from each window. Everything along the high road and in front of the inn was tranquil, where, contrary to the landlord's assertions, not a single light was discernible : the sound of the horn belonging to the night-guard was the only thing that interrupted the silence which universally prevailed.

Francis closed the windows, once again looked round the room, and, after snuffing the candles that they might burn the better, he threw himself on the bed, which he found good and comfortable; but although greatly fatigued, he could not get to sleep so soon as he had hoped. A slight palpitation of the heart, which he attributed to the agitation produced by the heat of his journey, kept him awake for a considerable time, till at length sleep came to his aid. After having, as he imagined, been asleep somewhat about an hour, he awoke and started up in a state of horror, possibly not unusual to a person whose blood is overheated; this idea in some degree allayed his apprehensions, and he listened attentively, but could hear nothing excepting the clock, which struck the hour of midnight. Again he listened for an instant, and turning on his side, he was just going off to sleep, when he fancied he heard a distant door grinding on its hinges, and then shut with a heavy noise. In an instant the idea of the ghost approaching caused him no little fear; but he speedily got the better of his alarm, by fancying it was only the wind: however, he could not comfort himself long with this belief, for the sound approached nearer and nearer, and resembled the clanking of chains, or the rattling of a large bunch of keys.

The terror which Francis experienced was beyond all description, and he put his head under the clothes. The doors continued to open with a frightful noise, and at last he heard some one trying different keys at the door of his room; one of them seemed perfectly to fit the lock, but the bolts kept the door fast; however, a violent shock like a clap of thunder caused them to give way, and in stalked a tall thin figure with a black beard, whose appearance was indicative of chagrin and melancholy : he was habited in the antique style, and on his left shoulder wore a red cloak or mantle, while his head was covered with a high-crowned hat. Three times, with slow and measured steps, he walked round the room, examined the consecrated candles, and snuffed them : he then threw off his cloak, unfolded a shaving apparatus, and took from it the razors, which he sharpened on a large leather strop hanging to his belt.

No powers are adequate to describe the agonies Francis endured : he recommended himself to the Virgin Mary, and endeavoured, as well as his fears would permit, to form an idea of the spectre's designs on him; whether he proposed to cut his throat, or only to take off his beard, he was at a loss to determine. The poor traveller, however, was a little more composed, when he saw the spectre take out a silver shaving pot, and in a basin of the same metal put some water; after which he made a lather, and then placed a chair; but a cold perspiration came over Francis, when the spectre, with a grave air, made signs for him to sit in that chair.

He knew it was useless to resist that mandate, which was but too plainly given; and thinking it most prudent to make a virtue of necessity, and to put a good face on the matter, Francis obeyed the order, jumped nimbly out of bed, and seated himself as directed.

The spirit placed the shaving-bib round his neck, then taking a comb and scissars, cut off his hair and whiskers; after which he lathered, according to rule, his beard, his eye-brows, and head, and shaved them

all off completely from his chin to the nape of his
neck. This operation ended, he washed his head,
wiped and dried it very nicely, made him a low bow,
folded up his case, put his cloak on his shoulder, and
made towards the door to go away.

The consecrated candles had burnt most brilliantly
during the whole of this operation ; and by their clear
light Francis discovered, on looking into the glass, that
he had not a single hair remaining on his head. Most
bitterly did he deplore the loss of his beautiful brown
hair ; but he regained courage on remarking, that, however great the sacrifice, all was now over, and that the
spirit had no more power over him.

In effect, the ghost walked towards the door with as
grave an air as he entered; but after going a few steps,
he stopped, looked at Francis with a mournful air, and
stroked his beard.   He three times repeated this action ;
and was on the point of quitting the room, when Francis began to fancy he wanted something. With great
quickness of thought he imagined it might be that he
wished him to perform a like service for him to that
which he had just been executing on himself.

As the spectre, spite of his woe-begone aspect, appeared more inclined to raillery than gravity, and as his
proceedings towards Francis appeared more a species of
frolic than absolute ill treatment, the latter no longer
appeared to entertain any apprehension of him ; and in
consequence determined to hazard the adventure.   He
therefore beckoned the phantom to seat himself in the
chair.   It instantly returned, and obeyed : taking off its
cloak, and unfolding the case, it placed it on the table,

and seated itself in the chair, in the attitude of one about to be shaved. Francis imitated precisely all he had seen it do : he cut off its hair and whiskers, and then lathered its head. The spirit did not move an inch. Our barber's apprentice did not handle the razor very dexterously; so that having taken hold of the ghost's beard against the grain, the latter made a horrible grimace. Francis did not feel much assured by this action; however, he got through the job as well as he could, and rendered the ghost's head as completely bald as his own.

Hitherto the scene between the two performers had passed in profound silence; but on a sudden it was interrupted by the ghost exclaiming, with a smiling countenance :—" Stranger, I heartily thank you for the eminent service you have rendered me ; for to you I am indebted for deliverance from my long captivity. During the space of three hundred years I have been immured within these walls, and my soul has been condemned to submit to this chastisement as a punishment for my crimes, until some living being had the courage to exercise retaliation on me, by doing to me what I have done by others during my life.

" Count Hartmann formerly resided in this castle ; he was a man who recognized no law nor superior; was of an arrogant and overbearing disposition; committed every species of wickedness, and violated the most sacred rights of hospitality; he played all sorts of malicious tricks to strangers who sought refuge under his roof, and to the poor who solicited his charity. I was his barber, and did everything to please him. No sooner did I perceive a pious pilgrim, than in an endearing tone I urged him to come into the castle, and prepared a bath for him; and while he was enjoying the idea of being taken care of, I shaved his beard and head quite close, and then turned him out of the bye-door, with raillery and ridicule. All this was seen by count Hartmann from his window with a sort of devilish pleasure, while the children would assemble round the abused stranger, and pursue him with cries of derision.

" One day there came a holy man from a far distant country; he wore a penitentiary cross at his back, and his devotion had imprinted scars on his feet, hands, and sides : his head was shaved, excepting a circle of hair, left to resemble the crown of thorns worn by our Saviour. He asked some water to wash his feet as he passed by, and some bread to eat. I instantly put him into the bath; but did not respect even *his* venerable head; upon which the pilgrim pronounced this terrible curse upon me : ' Depraved wretch,' said he, ' know that at your death, the formidable gates of heaven, of hell, and of purgatory, will alike be closed against your sinful soul, which shall wander through this castle, in the form of a ghost, until some man, without being invited or constrained, shall do to you what you have so long done to others.'

" From that moment the marrow in my bones dried up, and I became a perfect shadow; my soul quitted my emaciated body, which remained wandering within these walls, according to the prediction of the holy man. In vain did I look and hope for release from the painful ties which held me to earth; for know, that no sooner is the soul separated from the body, than it aspires to the blissful regions of peace, and the ardour of its wishes causes years to appear as long as centuries, while it languishes in a strange element. As a punishment, I was compelled to continue the trade that I had exercised during my life; but, alas! my nocturnal appearance soon rendered this castle deserted. Now and then a poor pilgrim entered to pass the night here: when they did, however, I treated them all as I have done you, but not one has understood me, or rendered me the only service which could deliver my soul from this sad servitude; henceforth, no spirit will haunt this castle, for I shall now enjoy that repose of which I have been so long in search. Once again let me thank you, gallant youth, and believe, that had I power over the hidden treasures of the globe, I would give them all to you; but, unfortunately, during my life riches did not fall to my lot, and this castle contains no store: however, listen to the advice I am now about to give you.

" Remain here till your hair is grown again, then return to your own country, and at that period of the year when the days and nights are of equal length, go on the bridge which crosses the Weser, and there remain till a friend, whom you will there meet, shall tell you what you ought to do to get possession of terrestrial wealth. When you are rolling in riches and prosperity, remember me, and on every anniversary of the day on which you released me from the heavy maledictions which overwhelmed me, cause a mass to be said for the repose of my soul. Adieu! I must now leave you."

Thus saying, the phantom vanished, and left his liberator perfectly astonished at the strange history he had just related. For a considerable time Francis remained immoveable, and reasoned with himself as to the reality of what he had seen ; for he could not help fancying still that it was only a dream : but his closely shaved head soon convinced him that the event had actually taken place. He got into bed again, and slept soundly until mid-day.

The malicious inn-keeper had been on the watch from the dawn of day for the appearance of the traveller, in order that he might enjoy a laugh at his expence, and express his surprise at the night's adventure. But after waiting till his patience was nearly exhausted, and finding it approaching to noon, he began to apprehend that the spirit had either strangled the stranger, or that he had died of fright. He therefore called his servants together, and ran with them to the castle, passing through every room till he reached the one in which he had observed the light the over night : there he found a strange key in the door, which was still bolted, for Francis had drawn the bolts again after the ghost had vanished. The landlord, who was all anxiety, knocked loudly ; and Francis, on awaking, at first thought it was the phantom come to pay him a second visit ; but at length recognising the landlord's voice, he got up and opened the door.

The landlord, affecting the utmost possible astonishment, clasped his hands together, and exclaimed, " Great God and all the saints ! then the *red cloak* has actually been here and shaved you completely ? I now see that the story was but too well founded. But pray relate to me all the particulars : tell me what the spirit was like: how he came thus to shave you, and what he said to you?"

Francis, having sense enough to discover his roguery, answered him by saying : "The spirit resembled a man wearing a red cloak; you know full well how he performed the operation: and his conversation I perfectly remember;—listen attentively:—' Stranger,' said he to me, ' do not trust to a certain inn-keeper, who has a figure of malice for his sign : the rogue knew well what would happen to you. Adieu ! I now quit this abode, as my time is come : and in future no spirit will make its appearance here. I am now about to be transformed into a night-mare, and shall constantly torment and haunt this said inn-keeper, unless he does penance for his villainy, by lodging, feeding, and furnishing you with everything needful, till your hair shall grow again, and fall in ringlets over your shoulders.' "

At these words the landlord was seized with a violent trembling: he crossed himself, and vowed to the Virgin Mary, that he would take care of the young stranger, lodge him, and give him every thing he required free of cost. He then conducted him to his house, and faithfully fulfilled what he promised.

The spirit being no longer heard or seen, Francis was naturally looked on as a conjuror: he several times passed a night in the castle, and one evening a courageous villager accompanied him, and returned without having lost his hair. The lord of the castle, hearing that the formidable *red cloak* was no longer to be

seen, was quite delighted; and gave orders that the
stranger who had delivered him from this spirit should
be well taken care of.

Early in the month of September Francis's hair began
to form into ringlets, and he prepared to depart; for all
his thoughts were directed towards the bridge over the
Weser, where he hoped, according to the barber's pre-
dictions, to find the friend who would point out to him
the way to make his fortune.

When Francis took leave of the landlord, the latter
presented him with a handsome horse well appointed,
and loaded with a large cloak-bag on the back of the
saddle, and gave him, at the same time, a sufficient sum
of money to complete his journey. This was a present
from the lord of the castle, expressive of his thanks
for having his castle again rendered habitable.

Francis arrived at his native place in high spirits:
he returned to his lodging in the little street, where he
lived very retired, contenting himself for the present
with secret information respecting Meta. All the
tidings he thus gained were of a satisfactory nature;
but he would neither visit her, nor make her acquainted
with his return, till his fate was decided.

He waited with the utmost impatience for the equi-
nox; till which, time seemed immeasurably long. The
night preceding the eventful day he could not close his
eyes to sleep, and that he might be sure of not missing
the friend with whom as yet he was unacquainted, he
took his station ere sun-rise on the bridge, where no
human being but himself was to be discovered: re-
plete with hopes of future good fortune, he formed a

thousand projects in what way to spend his money. Already had he, during the space of an hour, traversed the bridge alone, giving full scope to his imagination; when on a sudden the bridge presented a moving scene, and amongst others, many beggars took their several stations on it, to levy contributions on the passengers. The first of this tribe who asked charity of Francis was a poor devil with a wooden leg, who, being a pretty good physiognomist, judged from the gay and contented air of the young man, that his request would be crowned with success; and his conjecture was not erroneous, for he threw a demi-florin into his hat.

Francis, meanwhile, feeling persuaded that the friend he expected must belong to the highest class of society, felt no surprise at not seeing him at so early an hour, and waited therefore with patience. But as the hour for visiting the Exchange and Courts of Justice drew near, his eyes were in constant motion. He discovered at an immense distance every well-dressed person who came on the bridge, and his blood was in a perfect ferment as each approached him, for in some one of them did he hope to discover the author of his good fortune: but in vain he looked people in the face, no one paid attention to him. The beggars, who at noon were seated on the ground eating their dinner, remarking that the young man they had seen from the first of the morning, was the only person remaining with them on the bridge, and that he had not spoken to any one, nor appeared to have any employment, took him for a lazy vagabond; and although they had received marks of his beneficence, they began to make game of him, and,

R

in derision, called him the *provost* of the bridge.   The
physiognomist with the wooden leg observed, that his
air was no longer so gay as in the morning, and that,
having drawn his hat over his face, he appeared entirely
lost in thought, for he walked slowly along, nibbling
an apple, with an abstracted air.   The observer, resolving to benefit by what he had remarked, went to
the further extremity of the bridge, and after well
examining the visionary, came up to him as a stranger,
asked his charity, and succeeded to his utmost wish ;
for Francis, without turning round his head, gave him
another demi-florin.

In the afternoon a crowd of new faces presented
themselves to Francis's observation, while he became
quite weary at his friend's tardiness; but hope still
kept up his attention.   However, the fast declining
sun gave notice of the approach of night, and yet
scarcely any of the many passers-by had noticed
Francis ; some few, perhaps, had returned his salutation, but not one had, as he expected and hoped, embraced him : at length the day so visibly declined that
the bridge became nearly deserted, for even the beggars
went away.   A profound melancholy seized the heart
of poor Francis, when he found his hopes thus deceived ; and giving way to despair, he would have
precipitated himself into the Weser, had not the recollection of Meta deterred him.   He felt anxious, ere he
terminated his days in so tragical a manner, to see her
once again as she went to mass, and feast on the contemplation of her features.

He was preparing to quit the bridge when the beggar

with the wooden leg accosted him, for he had in vain puzzled his brains to discover what could possibly have caused the young man to remain on the bridge from morning till night. The poor cripple had waited longer than usual on account of Francis, in order to see when he went; but as he remained longer than he wished, curiosity at length induced him openly to address him, in order to learn what he so ardently desired to know.

" Pray excuse me, worthy sir," said he, " and permit me to ask you a question."

Francis, who was by no means in a mood to talk, and who now heard from the mouth of a beggar the words which he had so anxiously expected from a friend, answered him in rather an angry tone—" Well then, what is it you want to know, old man ?"

" Sir, you and I were the two first persons on this bridge to-day, and here we are still the only remaining two: as for me and my companions, it is pretty clear that we only come to ask alms; but it is equally evident you do not belong to our profession, and yet you have not quitted the bridge the whole day. My dear sir, for the love of God, if it is no secret, tell me, I entreat you, for what purpose you came, and what is the grief that rends your heart ?"

" What can it concern you, old dotard, to know where the shoe pinches me, or what afflictions I am labouring under ?"

" My good sir, I wish you well; you have twice bestowed your charity on me, which I hope the Almighty will return to you with interest. I could not but observe, however, that this evening your countenance no longer looked gay and happy as in the morning; and, believe me, I was sorry to see the change."

The unaffected interest evinced by the old man pleased Francis. "Well," replied he, "since you attach so much importance to the knowledge of the reason I have for remaining the whole day here plaguing myself, I will inform you that I came in search of a friend who appointed to meet me on this bridge, but whom I have expected in vain."

"With your permission, I should say your friend is a rogue, to play the fool with you in this manner: if he had so served *me*, I should make him feel the weight of my crutch whenever I met him; for if he has been prevented from keeping his word by any unforeseen obstacle, he ought at least to have sent to you, and not have kept you here on your feet a whole day."

"And yet I have no reason to complain of his not coming, for he promised me nothing: in fact, it was only in a dream that I was told I should meet a friend here."

Francis spoke of it as a dream, because the history of the ghost was too long to relate.

"That alters the case," replied the old man: "Since you rest your hopes on dreams, I am not astonished at your being deceived. I have also had many dreams in my life; but I was never fool enough to pay attention to them. If I had all the treasures that have been promised me in dreams, I could purchase the whole city of Bremen; but I have never put faith in dreams, and have not taken a single step to prove whether they were true or false, for I know full well it would be useless trouble; and I am astonished that you should have lost so fine a day, which you might have employed so much more usefully, merely on the strength of a dream, which appears to me so wholly devoid of sense or meaning."

" The event proves the justness of your remark, old father, and that dreams generally are deceitful; but it is rather more than three months since I had a very circumstantial dream relative to my meeting a friend on this particular day, here on this bridge; and it was so clearly indicated that he should communicate things of the utmost importance, that I thought it worth while to ascertain whether this dream had any foundation in truth."

" Ah, sir, no one has had clearer dreams than my-self, and one of them I shall never forget. I dreamt, several years since, that my good angel stood at the foot of my bed, in the form of a young man, and ad-dressed me as follows :—' Berthold, listen attentively to my words, and do not lose any part of what I am about to say. A treasure is allotted you; go and secure it, that you may be enabled to live happily the rest of your days. To-morrow evening, when the sun is set-ting, take a pickaxe and spade over your shoulder, and go out of the city by the gate leading to Hamburgh; when you arrive facing the convent of St. Nicholas, you will see a garden, the entrance to which is orna-mented by two pillars : conceal yourself behind one of these until the moon rises, then push the door hard, and it will yield to your efforts : go without fear into the garden, follow a walk covered by a treillage of vines, and to the left you will see a great apple-tree: place yourself at the foot of this tree, with your face turned towards the moon, and you will perceive, at fifteen feet distance, two bushy rose-trees ; search between these two shrubs, and at the depth of about six feet you will discover a great flag-stone, which covers the treasure inclosed within an iron chest ; and although it is heavy and difficult to handle, do not regret the labour it will occasion you to move it from the hole where it now is.   You will be well rewarded for your pains and trouble, if you look for the key which is hid under the box.' "

Francis remained like one stupified at this recital; and certainly would have been unable to conceal his astonishment, if the darkness of the night had not favoured him.   The various particulars pointed out by the beggar, brought to his recollection a little garden which he had inherited from his father, and which garden was the favourite spot of that good man ; but possibly for that very reason it was not held in estimation by the son.   Melchoir had caused it to be laid out according to his own taste, and his son, in the height of his extravagance, had sold it at a very low price.

The beggar with his wooden leg was now become a very interesting personage to Francis, who perceived that he was the friend alluded to by the ghost in the castle of Rummelsbourgh.   The first impulse of joy would have led him to embrace the mendicant ; but he restrained his feelings, thinking it best not to communicate the result of his intelligence to him.

" Well, my good man," said he, " what did you when you awoke ? did you not attend to the advice given by your good angel?"

" Why should I undertake a hopeless labour ? It was only a vague dream ; and if my good angel was anxious to appear to me, he might choose a night when I am not sleeping, which occurs but too frequently ; but he has not troubled his head much about me, for if he had I should not have been reduced, as I now am, to his shame, to beg my bread."

Francis took from his pocket another piece of money and gave it to the old man, saying, " Take this to procure half a pint of wine, and drink it ere you retire to rest. Your conversation has dispelled my sorrowful thoughts ; do not fail to come regularly to this bridge, where I hope we shall meet again."

The old lame man, not having for a long while made so good a day's work, overwhelmed Francis with his grateful benedictions: they separated, and each went their way. Francis, whose joy was at its height from the near prospect of his hopes being realized, very speedily reached his lodging in the bye street.

The following [day he ran to the purchaser of the little garden, and proposed to re-purchase it; the latter, to whom this property was of no particular value, and who, indeed, began to be tired of it, willingly consented to part with it. They very soon agreed as to the conditions of the purchase, and went immediately to sign the contract: with the money he had found in his bag, as a gift from the lord of Rummelsbourgh, Francis paid down half the price: he then procured the necessary tools for digging a hole in the earth, conveyed them to the garden, waited till the moon was up, strictly adhered to the instructions given him by the old beggar, set to work, and without any unlucky adventure he obtained the hidden treasure.

His father, as a precaution against necessity, had buried this money, without any intention to deprive his son of this considerable portion of his inheritance; but, dying suddenly, he had carried the secret to his grave, and nothing but a happy combination of circumstances could have restored this lost treasure to its rightful owner.

The chest, filled with gold pieces, was too heavy for Francis to remove to his lodging without employing some person to assist him; and feeling unwilling to become a topic of general conversation, he preferred concealing it in the summer-house belonging to the garden, and fetching it at several times. On the third day the whole was safely conveyed to his lodging in the little back street.

Francis dressed himself in the best possible style, and went to the church to request that the priest would substitute for the prayers which had been previously offered up, a thanksgiving *for the safe return of a traveller to his native country, after having happily terminated his business.* He concealed himself in a corner, where, unseen, he could observe Meta. The sight of her gave him inexpressible delight, especially when he saw the beautiful blush which overspread her cheeks, and the brilliancy of her eyes, when the priest offered up the thanksgiving. A secret meeting took place, as had been formerly arranged; and so much was Meta affected by it, that any indifferent person might have divined the cause.

Francis repaired to the Exchange, set up again in business, and in a very short time had enough to do: his fortune each succeeding day becoming better known, his neighbours judged that he had had greater luck than sense in his journey to collect his father's debts. He hired a large house in the best part of the town, engaged clerks, and continued his business with laudable and indefatigable assiduity; he conducted himself with the utmost propriety and sagacity, and abstained from the foolish extravagances which had formerly been his ruin.

The re-establishment of Francis's fortune formed the general topic of conversation. Every one was astonished at the success of his foreign voyage: but in proportion to the spreading fame of his riches, did Meta's tranquillity and happiness diminish; for it appeared that her silent lover was now in a condition to declare himself openly, and yet he remained dumb, and only manifested his love by the usual rencontre on coming out of church; and even this species of rendezvous became less frequent, which appeared to evince a diminution of his affection.

Poor Meta's heart was now torn by jealousy, for she imagined that the inconstant Francis was offering up his vows to some other beauty. She had experienced secret transports of delight on learning the change of fortune of the man she loved, not from interested motives and the wish to participate in his bettered fortune herself, but from affection to her mother, who, since the failure of the match with the rich brewer, absolutely seemed to despair of ever enjoying happiness or comfort in this world. When she thought Francis faithless, she wished that the prayers put up for him in the church had not been heard, and that his journey had not been attended with such entire success; for had he been reduced to means merely sufficient to procure the necessaries of life, in all probability he would have shared them with her.

Mother Bridget failed not to perceive her daughter's uneasiness, and easily guessed the cause; for she had heard of her old neighbour's surprising return, and she knew he was now considered an industrious, intelligent merchant : therefore, she thought, if his love for her daughter was what it ought to be, he would not be thus tardy in declaring it, for she well knew Meta's sentiments towards him. However, feeling anxious to avoid the probability of wounding her daughter's feelings, she avoided mentioning the subject to her; but the latter, no longer able to confine her grief to her own bosom, disclosed it to her mother, and confided the whole to her.

Mother Bridget did not reproach her daughter for her past conduct, but employed all her eloquence to console her, and entreated her to bear up with courage under the loss of all her hopes. " You must resign him," said she : " you scorned at the happiness which presented itself to your acceptance, therefore you must now endeavour to be resigned at its departure. Experience has taught me that those hopes which appear the best founded, are frequently the most delusive; follow my example, and never again deliver up your heart. Do not reckon on any amelioration of your condition, and you will be contented with your lot : honour this spinning-wheel, which produces the means of your subsistence, and then fortune and riches will be immaterial to you—you may do without them."

Thus saying, mother Bridget turned her wheel round with redoubled velocity, in order to make up for the time lost in conversation. She spoke nothing but the truth to her daughter: for since the opportunity was gone by when she hoped it was possible to have regained her lost comforts, she had in such a manner simplified her present wants and projects of future life, that it was not in the power of destiny to produce any considerable derangement in them. But, as yet, Meta was not so great a philosopher; so that her mother's exhortations, consolations, and doctrines, produced a precisely different effect on her from what they were intended : Meta looked on herself as the destroyer of the flattering hopes her mother had entertained. Although she did not formally accept the offer of marriage proposed to her, and even then could not have reckoned on possessing beyond the common necessaries of life, yet, since she had heard the tidings of the great fortune obtained by the man of her heart, her views had become enlarged, and she anticipated with pleasure that, by her choice, she might realize her mother's wishes.

Now, however, this golden dream had vanished:

Francis would not come again, and indeed they even began to talk in the city of an alliance about to take place between him and a very rich young lady of Anvers. This news was a death-blow to poor Meta : she vowed she would banish him from her thoughts ; but still moistened her work with her tears.

Contrary, however, to her vow, she was one day thinking of the faithless one ; for whenever she filled her spinning-wheel she thought of the following distich, which her mother had frequently repeated to her to encourage her in her work :—

" Spin the thread well ; spin, spin it more ;
For you see your intended is now at the door."

Some one did in reality knock gently at the door, and mother Bridget went to see who it was. Francis entered, attired as for the celebration of a wedding. Surprise for a while suspended mother Bridget's faculties of speech : Meta, blushing deeply and trembling, arose from her seat, but was equally unable with her mother to say a word : Francis was the only one of the three who could speak, and he candidly declared his love, and demanded of Bridget the hand of her daughter. The good mother, ever attentive to forms, asked eight days to consider the matter, although the tears of joy which she shed, plainly evinced her ready and prompt acquiescence ; but Francis, all impatience, would not hear of delay : finding which, she, conformable to her duty as a mother, and willing to satify Francis's ardour, adopted a mid-way, and left the decision to her daughter. The latter, obeying the dictates of her heart, placed herself by the side of the object of her tenderest affection; and Francis, transported with joy, thanked her by a kiss.

The two lovers then entertained themselves with talking over the delights of the time when they so well communicated their sentiments by signs; Francis had great difficulty in tearing himself away from Meta, and such ' converse sweet,' but he had an important duty to fulfil.

He directed his steps towards the bridge over the Weser, where he hoped to find his old friend with the wooden leg, whom he had by no means forgotten, although he had delayed making the promised visit. The latter instantly recognised Francis; and no sooner saw him at the foot of the bridge, than he came to meet him, and shewed evident marks of pleasure at sight of him.

" Can you, my friend," said Francis to him, after returning his salutation, " come with me into the new town and execute a commission ? You will be well rewarded for your trouble."

" Why not ?—with my wooden leg I walk about just as well as other people; and, indeed, have an advantage over them, for it is never fatigued. I beg you, however, my good sir, to have the kindness to wait till the man with the grey great-coat arrives."

" What has this man in the grey great-coat to do with you ?"

" He every day comes, as evening approaches, and gives me a demi-florin; I know not from whom : it is not indeed always proper to learn all things, so I do not breathe a word.   I am sometimes tempted to believe that it is the devil, who is anxious to buy my soul ; but it matters little, I have not consented to the bargain, therefore it cannot be valid."

" I verily believe that grey surtout has some malice in his head; so follow me, and you shall have a quarter florin over and above the bargain."

Francis conducted the old man to a distant corner, near the ramparts of the city, stopped before a newly built house, and knocked at the door.   As soon as the door was opened, he thus addressed the old beggar— " You have procured a very agreeable evening for me in the course of my life ; it is but just, therefore, that I should shed some comfort over your declining days. This house, and everything appertaining thereto, belongs to you: the kitchen and cellar are both well stocked, there is a person to take care of you, and every day at dinner you will find a quarter-florin under your plate : it is now time for you to know that the man in the grey surtout is my servant, whom I every day sent with my alms till this house was ready to receive you.   You may, if you please, consider me as your guardian angel, since your good angel did not acquit himself uprightly in return for your gratitude."

Saying this, he made the old man go into his house, where the latter found everything he could possibly desire or want : the table was spread, and the old man was so much astonished at this unexpected good fortune, that he thought it must be a dream, for he could in no way imagine why a rich man should feel so much interest for a miserable beggar. Francis having again assured him that everything he saw was his own, a torrent of tears expressed his thanks; and before he could sufficiently recover from his astonishment to express his gratitude by words, Francis had vanished.

The following day mother Bridget's house was filled with merchants and shopkeepers of all descriptions, whom Francis had sent to Meta, in order that she might purchase and get ready everything she required for her appearance in the world with suitable *eclat.* Three weeks afterwards he conducted her to the altar. The splendour of the wedding far exceeded that of the *King of Hops:* mother Bridget enjoyed the satisfaction of adorning her daughter's forehead with the nuptial crown, and thereby obtained the accomplishment of all her desires, and was recompensed for her virtuous and active life: she witnessed her daughter's happiness with delight, and proved the very best of grandmothers to her daughter's children.

THE PRUSSIAN, AND THE BRONZE STATUE.

COUNT LIEUWEN, a favourite officer in the service of the deceased King of Prussia, had under his special patronage and tuition a young engineer of high talent, whose advancement to his notice had been solely due to his merits : his battalion, led by the Austrian general Clairfait, then on its march through the Low Countries towards France, was ordered to surprise a small village on the frontiers, in the enemy's possession. In the middle of the night, young Ewald entered his commander's tent, and informed him that a negociation had been begun by the chief magistrate of this district, to admit the Prussian soldiers into an ambuscade, by which they might surround the French stationed in the village of Altheim, and put them to the sword. " Sir," he added, " I am acquainted with a path through the thicket that skirts the church-yard, and by leading fifty chosen men through it, we may enclose the farm and out-houses in which these Frenchmen lodge, and force them to surrender, without the baseness of entering their host's gates in groupes, disguised as travellers, and massacreing them in their sleep. This vile provost has made the offer in hopes of a reward, for which he conditions privately, heedless of the bloodshed and ravage which our soldiery would spread among the poor villagers in the blindness of their fury."

" You are right," replied the Count, " and it will be well to gain this advantageous post without disgrace to our characters as Prussian soldiers, or outrage to the unoffending natives. Through whose means did this honourable offer come? For I suspect the communicant is willing to share the reward?" The young engineer cast down his eyes, and answered, after a short and graceful hesitation, " He is my enemy, my lord—forgive me if I do not name him."

Count Lieuwen's brow grew smooth. " Well, Lichtenstein," he said, with a tone of familiarity he seldom used except when his heart was touched, " well, there will be no surer way, I see, to secure both our military credit, and this poor village from plunder, than to give you the command of the affair. Choose your comrades, and conduct them; but how is it that you know the avenues of this obscure place so well?"

Ewald was silent a few moments, only because he was conscious of feelings likely to make his voice less firm: when he had stifled them, he replied, " To you, who know my humble birth, and have remedied it so kindly by your patronage, I need not be afraid to confess this village was my birth-place, and that farm which the provost intends to deliver up to-night, for the purpose of massacre and riot, is—or was—" He could not add his meaning, but Count Lieuwen felt it. Brushing a tear hastily from his eyes, the old soldier bade him take his detachment, and obtain possession of the place in the manner he deemed fittest. Ewald departed instantly, and returned in the morning to announce his complete success, without loss to the in-

s

habitants, and without the escape of a single French-man. He brought, besides, a valuable despatch, which his advanced guard had intercepted; and the Count, delighted with the important result of the affair, and with the generous spirit it had exhibited, offered his young lieutenant a thousand crowns, the sum for which the treacherous provost had negociated, gallantly say-ing, his sovereign would more willingly pay it as the recompence of a hazardous and well-performed duty, than as the premium of a traitor. " If," said the lieutenant, modestly, " your lordship thinks this poor village worth a thousand crowns to his majesty, I pray you to consider them due to my senior officer, Dorf-fen : your personal kindness induced you to waive his right, and to give me the command of last night's affair; yet it is just that he should have the price of what he deserved to win.——" He shall have it," an-swered Lieuwen, compressing his lips sternly, " but I now know who would have bought what you have won honestly."

The first care of this brave veteran, on his return to Berlin, was to lay the circumstance of this fact before the king : the consequence was Ewald's promotion, and before the war ceased he rose to rank even higher than Count Lieuwen; and the last favour his old com-mander asked at Court was, that his adopted son might be appointed his successor in the fortress of Plauen, which his age rendered him averse to govern longer. This high distinction was granted; and the king, to suit the new governor's title to his important office, added the rank of Baron to the Cross of the Black

Eagle, already worn by Ewald de Lichtenstein. These unexpected honours did not alter the temper of the young hero; still preserving the bland urbanity of Marshal Turenne, whose elevation he had imitated so successfully, he was proud to hear his comrades hint that he too was a miller's son, and always strove to remind them how much he resembled his noble predecessor in benevolence and grace. But when he had offered his grateful obeisance, he solicited permission to absent himself one month, before he assumed his new duties. Count Lieuwen's friendship, and the peaceable state of the country, made the royal assent easy, and Ewald de Lichtenstein left Berlin to dedicate this short interval to his private happiness.

But Ewald, with all the splendour of his professional success, had not altered the humility of that private happiness. He had no hope so dear to him as to return to the little village of Altheim, which ten years before he had preserved from destruction, and to claim the farmer's daughter with whom the first affections of his boyhood had been exchanged: during the various and busy vicissitudes of a soldier's life, no correspondence had been possible, and he had time to snatch only a short interview when he entered the village with a hostile detachment. He took with him one attendant, a soldier of his own regiment, but unacquainted with his birth-place, though sufficiently attached to his person to ensure the secresy he required; not from mean fear of exposing his humble origin, but from a generous wish to avoid displaying his new and self-acquired greatness. The journey was tedious to his fancy, though he travelled rapidly, for the pleasantest dreams of his youth were ready to be realized. His servant had orders to make no mention of his name or rank when he arrived at his place of destination, and the little village of Altheim came in sight, in all the beauty of a summer evening, and a happy man's imagination: as he entered it, however, he perceived that several cottages were in ruins, and the farm where Josephine had lived was half-unroofed, and its gardens full of grass. Ewald's heart misgave him, and his servant went on before to inquire who occupied it. Schwartz brought his master intelligence that the niece of the former occupier had married a farmer, whose speculations had ended in inn-keeping, but with little success. There was no other inn, and if there had been one, Ewald, notwithstanding his heart-burnings, would have chosen this. He renewed his cautions to his servant, and entered the miserable house, where the master sat surlily smoking his pipe in a kitchen with broken windows, and a hearth almost cold: to his courteous request for accommodation, this man, whose suitable name was Wolfenbach, hardly returned an answer, except throwing him the remnant of a chair, and calling loudly at the door for his wife. A woman in wretched apparel, bending under a load of sticks, crept from a ruined outhouse, and came fearfully towards him— " Bring a faggot, drone, and cook some fish," said her ruffian husband; " where is the bread I bought this morning, and the pitcher of milk ?"—" There was but little milk," she answered, trembling, " and I gave it to our child."—" Brute-ideot !" he muttered with a hideous oath, and pushed her forwards by a blow which Ewald's heart felt. That moment would have discovered him, if the innkeeper had not left the room to attend his servant; and Ewald, as he looked again on Josephine's face, had courage enough to restrain a confession which would have aggravated her misery. Perhaps she had been left desolate—perhaps her husband had been made brutal by misfortune—at all events, he had no right to blame a marriage which circumstances had not permitted him to prevent. She might have had no alternative between it and disgrace, or Wolfenbach might have possessed and seemed to deserve her choice better than himself: this last thought held him silent, as he sat with his face shaded near the fire. Josephine took but one glance at him, and another at the cradle where a half-starved infant lay, before she began her humble labours to prepare a supper. Ewald attempted to say something, but his voice, hoarse with emotion, appeared unknown to her, and she turned away with a look of repressed pride and shame; yet as she could not but observe the earnest gaze of the stranger, her cheek, flushing with conscious recollection, recovered some part of its former beauty, and Ewald had taken the infant on his knee when Wolfenbach returned. His guest overcame the horror which almost impelled him to throw from him the offspring of a ruffian so debased, intending to convey into its cradle some aid for the unhappy mother, which might suffice to comfort her wants, without betraying the giver. He hid a purse of gold within its wrapper, and gave it back to Josephine: while the father, murmuring at such pests, rebuked her slow cookery. But Ewald could not eat; and tasting the flask, to propitiate the brutal landlord, withdrew to the bed meant for him, and was seen no more.

Late on the following morning two men, as they passed near the remains of a spoiled hay-rack, perceived motion in it, and heard a feeble noise; they took courage to remove some part, and, led on by traces of blood, examined till they found a body yet warm with life, but wounded in a ghastly manner; they conveyed it to the village surgeon, and collected help to surround the house of Wolfenbach, whom they remembered to have seen on the road, mounted on a horse which had been observed the day before entering Altheim, with the wounded man and another stranger. Skill and care restored this unfortunate sufficiently to make his deposition: he named his master, and stated that the gloomy looks and eager questions of the innkeeper had alarmed him on the night of Ewald's arrival, especially when he was desired to sleep in a ruined out-house. He had left it, and applying his ear to a crevice in the house-door, heard Wolfenbach menacing his wife with death if she prevented or betrayed his search into the traveller's portmanteau, which had been left below; for probably, in the heedlessness of anguish, Ewald had not thought of attending to it: he also heard Josephine's timid expostulations, and the shriek of her child in its father's savage grasp, held perhaps as a hostage for her silence. He went to warn his master, and, by calling through the casement of the loft where he lay awake, drew him from his bed : the stroke of an axe felled him to the ground, and he remembered nothing more. The fate of Ewald might be easily surmised. Detachments of the peasants traversed the country round to gain intelligence of him without success, and, without knowing his claims on them as their countryman, were all eager in their zeal to trace a man of rank and honour. Couriers met them from Berlin, despatched to hasten his return; but after six months spent in the most earnest search, even his paternal friend Count Lieuwen despaired of seeing him more, and believed him the victim of a ferocious robber. Wolfenbach had been seized with the horses of Ewald and his servant, which he had taken to sell at the nearest fair, and could not attempt even a plausible account of them : his miserable wife was in a state of delirium which unfitted her to give coherent evidence; but, the subject of her ravings, the purse of gold found in her infant's cradle, and a ring dropped near the traveller's bed, were powerful presumptive proofs against her husband : the rifled portmanteau was also discovered in a well, and the axe stained with blood. Wolfenbach maintained an obstinate and contumelious silence, during a long trial, which ended in a sentence of death, received with acclamations by the populace: he was carried to the scaffold attended by no friend, and died without confession.

Count Lieuwen resumed the government of the fortress he had resigned, but not till he had urged repeated inquiries, and proffered large rewards for any trace of his lost favourite, without effect; and when; after some years had past, a public duty compelled him to visit the country in which Ewald had perished, he travelled hastily, and loathed the necessity which forced his equipage to rest at Altheim for a few hours. During this short stay, the master of the new inn found means to introduce himself, and beg his guest's attention to a rare curiosity which he possessed. Finding, from his valet's account, that this exhibition was a tax imposed on every traveller, the Count assented, and listened patiently to his host's history of a bronze statue found in a peat-bog, at a short distance, and from thence brought to his house. He went into the room where it was deposited, prepared to see some antique relic or cunning counterfeit; but he saw, with feelings that need not be told, the body of his beloved Ewald, in the travelling habit he had seen him wear, vitrified, by the power of the morass, to the semblance of a bronze statue. He stood a few moments aghast with astonishment and horror, not unmingled with gladness, at this testimony of the truth preserved by a special operation of nature—for on the forehead, and in the neck of the seeming statue, two deep seams rendered the fact of Ewald's violent death unquestionable; but he had presence of mind enough to suppress his agitation, and affecting to believe the innkeeper exhibited, as he supposed himself, a strange piece of ancient sculpture, gave him a much larger sum than had been expected, even from a nobleman of his known munificence, and carried off the prize. But he caused it to be conveyed to Berlin without noise, and made it no subject of conversation among his attendants.

Count Lieuwen's return to the metropolis was always

followed by banquets given to his friends, and on this occasion he celebrated his arrival among them, by inviting the chief nobility, and all the military officers who had shared and survived his campaigns. After supper, before any had departed, he spoke of a most rare specimen of sculpture which he had reserved for their last regale—" You all know," said he, " my tender affection for Ewald de Lichtenstein, my regret for his untimely loss, and my wish to preserve his memory. I think you will agree with me in that wish to erect a monument, if we could decorate it with a representation of him suitable to his merits and his fate; but though we all know his merits, where shall we find an artist able to give a symbol of his death, since we know neither the time nor circumstance?"

The Count cast his eyes round the table as he spoke, and met approving and earnest looks from all his companions except one, whose head was averted—" But," he added, rising after a short pause, " I think I have found a statue sufficient itself for his monument."

A curtain suddenly drawn aside discovered the bronze statue of Ewald, lying on a bier composed of black turf. A silence of surprise and awe was followed by exclamations of wonder at the exquisite symmetry of the figure, and at the expression of the countenance, so nearly resembling its usual character, excepting the half-closed eyes, and lips parted as in the pangs of death. Some gathered round to observe the accurate folds of the drapery, and recognised every part of his usual travelling apparel—" There is even the shape of the seal-ring he wore upon his finger," said one of

266   THE PRUSSIAN, ETC.

the spectators, " and here is the ribbon he received the day before his departure from the king—but where is the cross of the Black Eagle ?"

" In his grave," replied Count Lieuwen, fixing his eyes on a guest who had never spoken—that guest was Dorffen, the senior officer superseded by Ewald. He suddenly lifted up his head, and answered—" *It is not !*"—The terrible sound of his voice, the decision of his words, made the assembly fall back from him, leaving him alone standing opposite the corpse: his features wrought a few instants in convulsions, and his lips moved in unconscious mutterings. " Then," (said a voice from among the group,) " the murderer robbed him of the cross ?"

" No, no—I robbed him of nothing—he robbed me of my place and honour, and of that cross which I might have earned at Altheim—we met alone—we were man to man—it was night, but I won the cross fairly, and now let him take it back.

The self-accused murderer made a desperate effort to throw it from his breast, and fell, with his whole weight and a laugh of madness, at the foot of the bier—the crowd raised him, but he spoke no more. His last words were truth, as subsequent inquiry proved. Accident, or a hope of vengence, had led him to the neighbourhood of Ewald's village; they had met on the road, and fatal opportunity completed Dorffen's guilt : he was buried under the scaffold, and the bronze statue remained a monument of Ewald's fate and of retributive justice.

THE MARRIAGE GIFT; A GERMAN STORY.

> But do not so——I have four hundred crowns,
> * * * *
> Take that;——and He that doth the ravens feed,
> Yea, providently caters for the sparrow,
> Be comfort to my age!——Here is the gold;
> All this I give you.
>
> SHAKSPEARE.

OTTO VON D——, after an absence of several years, two of which he had spent in the luxurious capital of France, was recalled to his native Germany by the unexpected death of his father. He found the family estate involved in difficulties, chiefly occasioned by extravagance and mismanagement, which would have appeared inextricable to a mind possessing less energy than his own; but by at once adopting a system of curtailment and method, he soon succeeded in bringing matters into such a train, as not only enabled him to discharge the accumulated arrears of interest, but also gradually to reduce the principal debt with which his property had been improvidently burthened.

It was not until his mind was relieved of this first care, and he could uninterruptedly form his plans for the future, that Otto thought of choosing a companion who might share with him the sweets of life, and assist him in combatting its toils. He had left Adelaide, the youngest daughter of his neighbour Von

Z——, an interesting girl of fourteen ; on his return, he found her blooming in all the charms of youthful innocence ; and he was not slow in observing, as well in the hearty welcome of her parents, as in the tell-tale blush of the maiden herself, that his addresses would not be unacceptable. He therefore embraced an early opportunity to declare his sentiments; and, after the preliminaries usual on such occasions, the happy day was fixed, arrived, and was observed with all those ceremonies which the country people, in some parts of Germany, still religiously keep up, according to the good old custom of their forefathers.

· First came the wedding guests, conducting the bride, modestly clad in white, with a veil covering her face, and who were met on the lawn by the peasantry, preceded by the village musicians. The married women brought their offering of a cradle, and fine baby-linen spun by themselves; the lads presented a handsome plough and harness ; the maidens a snow-white lamb; and the children doves and flowers. Adelaide gave her hand to all in silence ; Otto spoke few but impressive words, and, on concluding, invited the whole party, in the name of the bride's father, to a collation and dance on the green, for which preparations had already been made.

The lamps were now lighted up, and the fiddle and pipe were sounding merrily under the sweet-scented linden-trees, when a foreign livery servant, whose coat was rather the worse for wear, made his appearance on the dancing place. His singular tones and strange gesticulations soon collected around him a troop of laughing villagers; but it was not without considerable difficulty gathered from the broken German of the orator (whose hands and feet were equally eloquent with his tongue,) that his master's carriage had been overturned in the neighbourhood, and that a wheel was broken to pieces, which he was anxious to have put to rights, in order that he might prosecute his journey.

" Who talks of mending wheels, or going further to-day?" hiccupped the bride's father, whose satisfaction at his daughter's good fortune had displayed itself at table in copious libations. " To-day, added he, patting his ample sides, " let all wheels go in shivers: no man shall pass this house to-day—you may tell your master so; but stay, you may as well take me to him."—So saying, and attended by a crowd of followers, he proceeded to the highway, where they soon perceived a small wax-cloth covered carriage lying upset on the road, one of its hinder-wheels being as effectually demolished, as if an axe had been used in the operation. A tall thin figure, dressed in a plain blue frock-coat, having his right arm in a sling, a patch over his left eye, and whose woe-begone looks imparted to his general appearance no distant resemblance to the knight of the rueful countenance, stood near the vehicle, holding a jaded rosinante by the bridle. No sooner did he perceive the party approaching, than, hastening towards them, he addressed their leader in French, with much politeness of manner and fluency of utterance. Unfortunately, however, old Z——'s court language had lain too long rusty, and the state of his ideas was too muddled to enable him to brush it up at the moment, so that he was obliged to make the stranger understand, more by signs than words, that he must not think of continuing his journey that day at least, but must remain with them as a wedding guest.

The invitation was accepted with many thanks; and the stranger, having caused his Sancho to wipe the dust from his hat and boots, put his collar to rights, and opened his surtout, under which a sort of uniform modestly peeped out : thus prepared, he set himself in motion by the help of a stout crutch stick, and it then further appeared that his left foot was also disabled, though there was something not ungraceful in its hobble. On reaching the linden-place, he requested to be introduced to the young couple, and after wishing the bridegroom joy, he kissed the bride's hand with the air of an old beau, and whispered many flattering things to her in his own language.

When this matter was settled, all hastened again to dance and play. Otto soon removed his bride to another quarter; and it seemed quite natural, that the stiff and wearied old man should choose his seat on a bench apart from persons who neither understood him nor he them.

On supper being announced, the stranger accompanied the rest to the eating apartment, where he planted himself, with considerable adroitness, between two of the rosiest and plumpest lasses in the room, to the no small mortification of a young lieutenant, who had fixed on this place for himself. Hilarity and mirth now presided over the happy party; the good-humoured joke was bandied about, and the hearty laugh echoed round the room, when one of the servants entered with a packet, which a messenger had just delivered, with directions that it should be given into the bridegroom's own hands. The curiosity of all was excited, and Otto was induced, by their solicitations, to open the packet immediately; and, after removing almost innumerable covers, he at length produced a plain wooden drinking-cup, with a silver rim, on which was engraved, " *Present de nôces du Gueux.*"

" Jaques!" cried Otto, kissing the cup with emotion. Adelaide cast an enquiring eye at her lover, and lifted up the cup to examine it more nearly; but she had scarcely raised it from the table, when its unexpected weight occasioning her to replace it rather smartly, the bottom fell out, and discovered a rose-coloured case, containing a pair of bracelets set in brilliants of the purest water, and newest fashion: the words " *à la belle epouse de mon ami,*" were embroidered on the satin.

The surprise and curiosity on all sides may be easily conceived: all the guests rose from their seats, except the stranger, who remained sitting with the most perfect indifference, and an expression of countenance that almost appeared to indicate contempt for what was going forward. Otto, whose growing dislike to the stranger was not lessened by this conduct, measured him with an eye of indignation, and allowed himself the more readily to be persuaded, by his bride and the other guests, to satisfy their enquiries.

" Yes !" he began, a fine glow suffusing his manly
cheeks ; " yes ! I am not ashamed to own it : a beggar
—Jaques is the worthy man's name—is my dearest
friend ; is, to express all to you in a few words, the
preserver of my life and honour.   However painful it
may be to me, on an occasion like the present, to accuse
myself of a youthful indiscretion, yet I shall not hesitate
to do so, as I cannot otherwise, perhaps, do justice to
the noble-minded Jaques, whose marriage-present shall
ever be dear to my heart, and the most valued ornament
of my Adelaide."

" Then let me wear it to-day," said the lovely girl,
with tremulous voice ; and the bracelets were quickly
transferred from their rose-coloured covering to the
white satin of her arms.   Otto resumed, after a short
pause :

" During my residence in Paris, I was almost daily in
the habit of passing along the Pont-Neuf.   At one end
of the bridge, and generally about the same spot, there
sat a beggar, who, although he seemed scarcely more
than fifty, had frequented the place upwards of thirty
years, and was commonly known by the name of ' old
Jaques.'   Not out of any feeling of compassion, but
merely because his general appearance rather interested
me, I threw a sous into his hat as often as I chanced to
pass near him.   This became, at length, so habitual to
me, that whenever I approached his station, I put my
hand involuntarily into my pocket.   He always wished
me every possible good — chatted with me, when I
was at leisure, about the news of the day — even
warned me now and then, against the dangers of the

town ; in short, in the course of half a year, we stood together on the footing of acquaintances, who, though of different rank, are yet mutually pleased with each other.

" My time in Paris was spent very agreeably, and, I may flatter myself, not altogether without advantage. I lived as decently as my means permitted, but never extravagantly, till, a short time before my departure, my evil stars brought me acquainted with some young men who were addicted to gambling, and who, by little and little, led me on to stake first small and then large sums at play: the consequence of this was as may be supposed ; but it was not until I had lost all my own money, and had become deeply indebted to my *soi-disant* friends, that I began seriously to reflect on my situation.

" I immediately formed the resolution to pause, ere it was too late, and quit the capital for ever, after discharging the debt which I had contracted. I therefore wrote to my father, requesting such a remittance as might be necessary for this purpose; but that letter, and several which I sent subsequently, remained unanswered : my bills, meanwhile, became due : I was forced to have recourse to the assistance of usurers, and ruin stared me in the face.

" Disheartened, gloomy, and silent, I now passed Jaques without noticing him : his fixed and earnest gaze became intolerable, and I avoided the place where he stood.

" At length I received the long-looked for letters from home; but instead of the remittances with which

T

I had hoped to silence the most clamorous of my creditors, they brought me the intelligence of my father's death, after a short illness, and announced the impossibility of sending me more money than would barely suffice for my travelling expenses.

" Nursed in the lap of affluence, and unused to privation of any sort, it may easily be supposed that I was but little prepared for such news. The death of my good father filled me with sorrow : the involved situation of his affairs, which I now learned for the first time, deprived me of all hope for the future. The idea of having debts which I could not discharge, and the prospect of prison in a foreign land, threw me into despair. The longer I considered, the more did my situation appear utterly hopeless, till, at length, in a state of mind bordering on frenzy, and with a determination which such a state only could inspire, I walked out, after a sleepless night, and bent my course towards the river. I was already within a few paces of the Pont Neuf, when Jaques threw himself, with greater importunity than usual, in my way. I *would* not see him.

" ' One word, Sir,' said he, in a tone of entreaty, and taking hold of the skirt of my coat. ' Leave me, old man,' said I, with forced composure; ' to-day I have given *all* away.' He guessed my meaning better than I intended he should. ' By all that's sacred, my dear young master !' said he, solemnly, ' confide in me : what has happened ?'

" ' What is that to thee ?' I replied ; ' thou canst not help me.'

" ' Who knows ? only speak, Sir ! I cannot rest until I learn what has so changed you. Tell me the cause of your dejection.'

" ' Why, only a paltry thousand louis !' said I, with a shrug.

" ' And *is* that all ? Good ! I will lend them to you.'

" ' You, Jaques ! Good old man, you have been drinking too freely this morning.'

" Well, only take the trouble of coming to me to-night ; and, till then, I conjure you, do nothing rashly.'

" The earnestness of his manner, the firmness with which he spoke, and the reflection that I could at any time carry my intention into effect, brought my thoughts into another channel, and induced me to yield to his request. Jaques gave me his address, in a remote suburb, and I pledged my word of honour to meet him there the same evening.

" Urged by curiosity, more than by hope, I appeared at the appointed time and place, and found Jaques in a small but extremely clean apartment, plain but neatly furnished ; he now wore a decent coat, and came forward to meet me with a friendly look.

" ' Consider all that you see here as your own,' said he. ' I have neither child nor relation, and what I daily receive from the benevolent, suffices for my own and my housekeeper's wants.'

" Little as I had calculated on the old man's assistance, yet this address appeared too ridiculous ; and I was hesitating whether I should consider him a fool or a madman, when he at once put an end to my doubts ;

T 2

for, requesting me to partake of the refreshments
which he had provided, he raised a part of the floor,
and brought from underneath a heavy wooden vessel,
which he placed with difficulty on the table; on removing the lid, you may figure my astonishment when
I saw that it was filled to the brim with gold pieces.

" ' Help yourself, Sir,' said he, smiling : ' here are
about twelve hundred louis : it is all I have by me in
ready cash ; but I soon can procure more.'

" ' Do not mistake me,' continued my honest Jaques ;
' I am no common beggar, who drive the trade from
love of idleness, and cheat the needy of the charitable
gift of the compassionate : I am of noble though poor
birth.   Having lost my parents early, I entered the
army in my sixteenth year, served under the great
Saxe, and if worthy of such a leader let this testify :'
a cross of St. Louis lay on the heap of gold.   ' In my
twentieth year, a cannon-shot carried away my right
arm : I received my discharge, and was thrown on the
world destitute and hopeless.   Ignorant of any trade
by which I could gain a livelihood, and rendered incapable of labour by the loss of my arm, I abandoned
myself to a profound melancholy, which threw me into
a long and severe illness; when I recovered, my disappointed prospects, and a sort of spite at the world,
made me a beggar; my youth and infirmities gained
me more compassion than I had expected, and I soon
earned not only my daily subsistence, but became enabled to lay by a trifle daily, which, by little and little,
amounted to a considerable sum. Out of this I assisted
such of my companions in misery as had been less

fortunate than myself in this calling, and thereby acquired a sort of consideration amongst them, but no disinterested attachment: this vexed me. I adopted a foundling as my own child, and began to live even more sparingly than before, in order to make provision for him: I had him carefully brought up and educated, till his sixteenth year, when a counseller was pleased with the lad, and took him into his service. This very boy—O François, François, how many tears have I shed on thy account!—soon began to consider it beneath him to be on terms of intimacy with a beggar; and on the same day that you first gave me an alms, he had the cruelty to pass as if he did not know me. He was ashamed of me—of *me*, who at that moment was begging to make him independent. 'He heeds me not,' said I; and his unnatural conduct drove all the blood to my heart. 'Thou all-powerful Being! give me then another son.' Scarcely had I uttered the prayer when you approached, and threw, with a compassionate look, a gift into my hat."

Otto was moved even to tears, and was forced to make a pause.

" ' *You* will not be ashamed of me,' continued Jaques. ' You are now unfortunate: make the old beggar happy by accepting his assistance.'

" You may easily imagine how I felt at this moment. The wonderful intervention of Providence, to prevent the commission of a crime at which I shudder; the noble, I may say the heavenly look of the good old man; but, above all, my own dreadful situation, crowded into my thoughts, and I did not hesitate to avail myself of his generous offer. My intention of disclosing to him the cause of my embarrassments was needless, for he had already informed himself of every particular.

" I allowed him to count out one thousand louis, and then requested pen and ink, in order to give him an acknowledgment for the amount; but my benefactor would not hear a word of this, ' Take,' said he, 'as much as you require; and if you die,' added he, ' you can pay me yonder! I want but little here. *You* are sent to me as a son, whether you will or no; and you, at least, cannot deprive me of the secret satisfaction of being your father.'

" ' Yes, father! preserver and father,' cried I, falling on his bosom, ' Nature gave me one, and when I lost him, heaven replaced him in you.'

" I did not leave Jaques's cottage till a late hour, when I returned home with a lightened heart, and refreshing sleep once more visited my eyelids.

" Early on the following day I paid off every creditor, had another *tête-à-tête* with Jaques, and prepared immediately to quit France. My first care, on arriving here, would most certainly have been to discharge this, which I could truly call a debt of honour ; but as he had expressly required me, at parting, not to think of this till after the end of a year at soonest, to give him, as he said, a proof of confidence, I deferred doing so till very lately, when, on repaying him his loan, I had the satisfaction of acquainting him with my approaching union."

" And he shall be *my* father also," said Adelaide, pressing his hand : then rising, and filling the goblet with wine, " Let us drink to the health of my worthy fathers, John Von Z——, and Jaques the beggar!"

Every one present pledged the toast with enthusiasm except the old stranger, who, still evincing the most cutting indifference, pushed his chair back, and hastily rose up, with a countenance on which was written, in pretty legible characters, ' What a fuss about a beggar!'

" Sir, you abuse the rights of hospitality!" cried Otto, angrily, and going up to the Frenchman, with the determination of making him quit the apartment.

" Mon ami, ah, mon fils !" replied the old man, with the tenderest expression, and removing, at the same time, the bandage from his left eye, " now, indeed, I am satisfied that my choice has not been misplaced : you have not been ashamed to acknowledge the old beggar ; your lovely bride, too, has called me father : for this alone have I undertaken a long journey, and caused my carriage to be overturned at your gate." He was now, in his turn, overcome ; all the guests crowded round him with praises and caresses ; and the grateful Otto, kissing his Adelaide, called this the happiest day of his life.

" Only allow me to pass my few remaining years with you," added Jaques, as he drew from his bosom a packet with his left hand, it being now remarked by all that the right was skilfully formed of wax. " There, my son, are your papers back. I will never be a burthen to you. I have twelve hundred livres yearly of rent; all I request is a small apartment in your house, or wheresoever else an honest beggar may patiently wait his end."

Otto tenderly embraced his adopted father, and the wooden cup was frequently replenished in the course of the evening.

ZERLINA, AND THE OWL OF THE ARNO.

An indiscreet friend, says the proverb, is more dangerous than the naked sword of an enemy; and, truly, there is nothing more fatal than the act of a misjudging ally, which, like a mistake in medicine, is apt to kill the unhappy patient it was intended to cure.

This lesson was taught, in a remarkable manner, to the innocent Zerlina, a peasant; to conceive which, you must suppose her to have gone, by permission, into the garden of the Countess of Marizzo, near the Arno, one beautiful morning of June. It was a spacious pleasure ground, excellently disposed, and adorned with the choicest specimens of shrubs and trees, being bounded, on all sides, by hedge-rows of laurels and myrtles, and such sombre evergreens, and in the midst was a pretty verdant lawn, with a sun-dial. The numberless plants that belong to that bountiful season were then in full flower, and the delicate fragrance of the orange blossoms perfumed the universal air. The thrushes were singing, merrily, in the copses; and the bees, that cannot stir without music, made a joyous humming with their wings. All things were vigorous and cheerful, except one, a poor owl, that had been hurt by a bolt from a cross-bow, and so had been unable, by daylight, to regain its accustomed hermitage, but sheltered itself under a row of laurel trees and hollies, that afforded a delicious shadow in the noon-tide sun. There, shunning and shunned by all, as it is the lot of the unfortunate, he languished over his wound, till a flight of pert sparrows espying him, he was soon forced to endure a thousand twittings, as well as buffets, from that insolent race. The noise of these chatterers attracting the attention of Zerlina, she crossed over to the spot, and, lo! there crouched the poor bewildered owl, blinking with his large bedazzled eyes, and nodding as if with giddiness from his buffetings, and the blaze of unusual light. The tender girl, being very gentle and compassionate by nature, was no way repelled by its ugliness, but, thinking only of its sufferings, took up the feathered wretch in her arms, and endeavoured to revive it, by placing it on her bosom. There, nursing it with an abundance of pity and concern, she carried it to the grass plat, and, being ignorant of its habits, laid out the poor drooping bird, as her own lively spirits prompted her, in the glowing sunshine; for she felt in her own heart, at that moment, the kind and cheerful influence of the genial sun. Then, withdrawing a little way, and leaning against the dial, she awaited the grateful change which she hoped to behold in the creature's looks; whereas, the tormented owl, being grievously dazzled, and annoyed more than ever, hopped off again, with many piteous efforts, to the shady evergreens. Notwithstanding, believing that this shyness was only because of its natural wildness, or fear, she brought it back again to the lawn, and then, running into the house for some crumbs to feed it withal, the poor old owl, in the meantime, crawled partly back, as before, to its friendly shelter of holly.

The simple girl found it, therefore, with much wonder, again retiring towards those gloomy bushes. Why, what a wilful creature is this, she thought, that is so loth to be comforted. No sooner have I placed it in the warm cheerful sunshine, which enlivens all its fellow birds to chirp and sing, than it goes back, and mopes under the most dismal corners. I have known many human persons to have those peevish fits, and to reject kindness as perversely ;—but who would look for such unnatural humours in a simple bird ? Wherewith, taking the monkish fowl from its dull leafy cloisters, she disposed him once more on the sunny lawn, where it made still fresh attempts to get away from the over-painful radiance, but was now become too feeble and ill to remove. Zerlina, therefore, began to believe that it was reconciled to its situation ; but she had hardly cherished this fancy, when a dismal film came suddenly over its large round eyes, and then, falling over upon its back, after one or two slow gasps of its beak, and a few twitches of its aged claws, the poor martyr of kindness expired before her sight. It cost her a few tears to witness the tragical issue of her endeavours ; but she was still more grieved, afterwards, when she was told of the cruelty of her unskilful treatment ; and the poor owl, with its melancholy death, were the frequent subject of her meditations.

In the year after this occurrence, it happened that the Countess of Marizzo was in want of a young female attendant, and, being much struck with the modesty and lively temper of Zerlina, she requested her parents to let her live with her. The poor people, having a numerous family to provide for, agreed very cheerfully to the proposal, and Zerlina was carried by her benefactress to Rome. Her good conduct confirming the prepossessions of the countess, the latter showed her many marks of her favour and regard, not only furnishing her handsomely with apparel, but taking her as a companion on her visits to the most rich and noble families, so that Zerlina was thus introduced to much gaiety and splendor. Her heart, notwithstanding, ached oftentimes under her silken dresses, for, in spite of the favour of the countess, she met with many slights from the proud and wealthy, on account of her humble origin, as well as much envy and malice from persons of her own condition. She fell, therefore, into a deep melancholy, and, being interrogated by the countess, she declared that she pined for her former humble, but happy, estate; and begged, with all humility, that she might return to her native village.

The countess being much surprised, as well as grieved, at this confession, inquired if she had ever given her cause to repent of her protection? To which Zerlina replied, with many grateful tears, but still avowing the ardour of her wishes, "Let me return," said she, "to my homely life,—this oppressive splendor dazzles and bewilders me. I feel, by a thousand humiliating misgivings and disgraces, that it is foreign to my nature; my defects of birth and manners making me shrink continually within myself, while those who were born for its blaze perceive, readily, that I belong to an obscure race, and taunt me with jests and indignities for intruding on their sphere; those also who should be my equals, are quite as bitter against me, for overstepping their station, so that my life is thus a round of perpetual mortifications and uneasiness: pray, therefore, absolve me of ingratitude, if I long to return to my native and proper shades, with their appointed habits: I am dying, like the poor owl, for lack of my natural obscurity." The curiosity of the countess being awakened by the last expression, Zerlina related to her the story of that unfortunate bird, and applied it, with a very touching commentary, to her own condition, so that the countess was affected even to the shedding of tears. She immediately comprehended the moral, and carrying back Zerlina to her native village, she bestowed her future favour so judiciously, that, instead of being a misfortune, it secured the complete happiness of the pretty peasant.

FINIS.

LONDON: PRINTED BY J. TRAPP AND CO. BUDGE ROW.

CPSIA information can be obtained
at www.ICGtesting.com
Printed in the USA
BVHW081742260819
556820BV00004B/309/P

9 781406 990218